2024 Ninja Dual Zone Cookbook UK For Beginners

2500 Days Fast & Tasty and Healthy 2-Basket Air Fryer Recipes for Your Ninja Dual Zone Air Fryer

Merlin E. Williford

All rights reserved worldwide.

No part of this book may be reproduced or transmitted in any form or by any means, electronic or mechanical, including photo copying, recording or by any information storage and retrieval system, without written permission from the publisher, except for the inclusion of brief quotations in a review.

Warning-Disclaimer:

The purpose of this book is to educate and entertain. The author or publisher does not guarantee that anyone following the techniques, suggestions, tips, ideas, or strategies will become successful. The author and publisher shall have neither liability or responsibility to anyone with respect to any loss or damage caused, or alleged to be caused, directly or indirectly by the information contained in this book.

CONTENTS

MEASUREMENT CONVERSIONS 9

Breakfast Recipes 11

Breakfast Stuffed Peppers 11
Yellow Potatoes With Eggs 11
Bacon Cinnamon Rolls 12
Sweet Potato Hash 12
Cheesy Baked Eggs 13
Sausage With Eggs 13
Homemade Toaster Pastries 14
Brussels Sprouts Potato Hash 14
Cajun Breakfast Sausage 15
Double-dipped Mini Cinnamon Biscuits 15
Quick And Easy Blueberry Muffins 16
Broccoli-mushroom Frittata And Chimichanga Breakfast Burrito 16
Bacon-and-eggs Avocado And Simple Scotch Eggs 17
Puff Pastry 18
Spinach And Swiss Frittata With Mushrooms 18
Breakfast Sausage And Cauliflower 19
French Toast Sticks 19
Red Pepper And Feta Frittata 20
Pork Sausage Eggs With Mustard Sauce 20
Bacon Cheese Egg With Avocado And Potato Nuggets 21
Easy Sausage Pizza 21
Bacon And Eggs For Breakfast 22
Breakfast Frittata 22
Mushroom-and-tomato Stuffed Hash Browns 23
Donuts 23
Onion Omelette And Buffalo Egg Cups 24
Sausage And Egg Breakfast Burrito 24

Sweet Potato Sausage Hash 25
Wholemeal Banana-walnut Bread 26

Fish And Seafood Recipes 26

Easy Herbed Salmon 26
Crispy Parmesan Cod 27
Herb Lemon Mussels 27
Rainbow Salmon Kebabs And Tuna Melt 28
Dukkah-crusted Halibut 28
"fried" Fish With Seasoned Potato Wedges 29
Simple Buttery Cod & Salmon On Bed Of Fennel And Carrot 30
Honey Teriyaki Tilapia 30
Fish Sandwich 31
Fish Fillets With Lemon-dill Sauce 31
Tilapia With Mojo And Crispy Plantains 32
Keto Baked Salmon With Pesto 33
Tandoori Prawns 33
Scallops With Greens 34
Crumb-topped Sole 34
Salmon Nuggets 35
Thai Prawn Skewers And Lemon-tarragon Fish En Papillote 35
Air Fryer Calamari 36
Nutty Prawns With Amaretto Glaze 37
Furikake Salmon 37
Prawns Curry And Paprika Crab Burgers 38
Salmon Patties 39
Cod With Jalapeño 39
Tuna With Herbs 40
Scallops Gratiné With Parmesan 40
Chili Lime Tilapia 41
Pecan-crusted Catfish Nuggets With "fried" Okra 41
Oyster Po'boy 42
Miso Salmon And Oyster Po'boy 43

Seasoned Tuna Steaks 44

Poultry Recipes 44

Honey Butter Chicken 44
Pecan-crusted Chicken Tenders 45
Crumbed Chicken Katsu 45
Asian Chicken Drumsticks 46
Stuffed Chicken Florentine 46
Bbq Cheddar-stuffed Chicken Breasts 47
Cornish Hen With Baked Potatoes 47
Harissa-rubbed Chicken 48
Ranch Turkey Tenders With Roasted Vegetable Salad 48
Indian Fennel Chicken 49
Tex-mex Chicken Roll-ups 50
Almond Chicken 50
Crispy Ranch Nuggets 51
Greek Chicken Meatballs 51
Buffalo Chicken 52
Crusted Chicken Breast 52
Chipotle Drumsticks 53
Thai Chicken Meatballs 53
Greek Chicken Souvlaki 54
Chicken Bites 54
Hawaiian Chicken Bites 55
Chicken & Broccoli 55
Chicken Thighs In Waffles 56
Easy Cajun Chicken Drumsticks 56
Cornish Hen With Asparagus 57
Yummy Chicken Breasts 57
Turkey Meatloaf With Veggie Medley 58

Beef, Pork, And Lamb Recipes 59

Stuffed Beef Fillet With Feta Cheese 59

Mojito Lamb Chops 59

Spice-rubbed Pork Loin 60

Steak And Asparagus Bundles 60

Rosemary Ribeye Steaks And Mongolian-style Beef 61

Chorizo And Beef Burger 62

Lamb Chops With Dijon Garlic 62

Tasty Lamb Patties 63

Tomahawk Steak 63

Pork Chops With Brussels Sprouts 64

Cheesesteak Taquitos 64

Steaks With Walnut-blue Cheese Butter 65

Mozzarella Stuffed Beef And Pork Meatballs 65

Smothered Chops 66

Bacon Wrapped Pork Tenderloin 66

Italian Sausages With Peppers And Teriyaki Rump Steak With Broccoli 67

Spicy Lamb Chops 68

Steak Fajitas With Onions And Peppers 68

Asian Glazed Meatballs 69

Marinated Pork Chops 69

Parmesan Pork Chops 70

Roast Beef 70

Ham Burger Patties 71

Steak In Air Fry 71

Pork With Green Beans And Potatoes 72

Snacks And Appetizers Recipes 72

Fried Cheese 72

Pretzels Hot Dog 73

Waffle Fries 73

Potato Chips 74

Strawberries And Walnuts Muffins 74

Zucchini Chips 75

Beef Skewers 75
Cheese Stuffed Mushrooms 76
Chicken Crescent Wraps 76
Healthy Spinach Balls 77
Jalapeño Popper Chicken 77
Beef Jerky Pineapple Jerky 78
Crispy Filo Artichoke Triangles 78
Taco-spiced Chickpeas And Black Bean Corn Dip 79
Chicken Stuffed Mushrooms 80
Cheese Corn Fritters 80
Mexican Jalapeno Poppers 81
Crab Cake Poppers 81
Healthy Chickpea Fritters 82
Caramelized Onion Dip With White Cheese 82

Desserts Recipes 83

Sweet Potato Donut Holes 83
Delicious Apple Fritters 83
Chocó Lava Cake 84
Apple Crumble 84
Berry Crumble And S'mores 85
Air Fried Bananas 85
Mini Blueberry Pies 86
Pecan Brownies And Cinnamon-sugar Almonds 86
Pecan And Cherry Stuffed Apples 87
Gluten-free Spice Cookies 87
Molten Chocolate Almond Cakes 88
Stuffed Apples 88
Homemade Mint Pie And Strawberry Pecan Pie 89
Spiced Apple Cake 89
Butter Cake 90
Mini Strawberry And Cream Pies 91
Chocolate Chip Muffins 91

Jelly Donuts 92

Vegetables And Sides Recipes 92

Acorn Squash Slices 92

Quinoa Patties 93

Fried Olives 94

Garlic-rosemary Brussels Sprouts 94

Balsamic Vegetables 95

Green Beans With Baked Potatoes 95

Garlic-herb Fried Squash 96

Garlic Herbed Baked Potatoes 96

Fried Avocado Tacos 97

Falafel 97

Flavourful Mexican Cauliflower 98

Stuffed Tomatoes 99

Broccoli, Squash, & Pepper 99

Satay-style Tempeh With Corn Fritters 100

Fried Patty Pan Squash 101

Air-fried Radishes 101

Green Tomato Stacks 102

Buffalo Seitan With Crispy Zucchini Noodles 102

Chickpea Fritters 103

Air Fryer Vegetables 104

RECIPES INDEX 105

MEASUREMENT CONVERSIONS

BASIC KITCHEN CONVERSIONS & EQUIVALENTS

DRY MEASUREMENTS CONVERSION CHART

3 TEASPOONS = 1 TABLESPOON = 1/16 CUP
6 TEASPOONS = 2 TABLESPOONS = 1/8 CUP
12 TEASPOONS = 4 TABLESPOONS = 1/4 CUP
24 TEASPOONS = 8 TABLESPOONS = 1/2 CUP
36 TEASPOONS = 12 TABLESPOONS = 3/4 CUP
48 TEASPOONS = 16 TABLESPOONS = 1 CUP

METRIC TO US COOKING CONVER-SIONS

OVEN TEMPERATURES

120 °C = 250 °F
160 °C = 320 °F
180 °C = 350 °F
205 °C = 400 °F
220 °C = 425 °F

LIQUID MEASUREMENTS CONVERSION CHART

8 FLUID OUNCES = 1 CUP = 1/2 PINT = 1/4 QUART
16 FLUID OUNCES = 2 CUPS = 1 PINT = 1/2 QUART
32 FLUID OUNCES = 4 CUPS = 2 PINTS = 1 QUART
1/4 GALLON
128 FLUID OUNCES = 16 CUPS = 8 PINTS = 4 QUARTS = 1 GALLON

BAKING IN GRAMS

1 CUP FLOUR = 140 GRAMS
1 CUP SUGAR = 150 GRAMS
1 CUP POWDERED SUGAR = 160 GRAMS
1 CUP HEAVY CREAM = 235 GRAMS

VOLUME

1 MILLILITER = 1/5 TEASPOON
5 ML = 1 TEASPOON
15 ML = 1 TABLESPOON
240 ML = 1 CUP OR 8 FLUID OUNCES
1 LITER = 34 FL. OUNCES

WEIGHT

1 GRAM = 035 OUNCES
100 GRAMS = 3.5 OUNCES
500 GRAMS = 1.1 POUNDS
1 KILOGRAM = 35 OUNCES

US TO METRIC COOKING CONVERSIONS

1/5 TSP = 1 ML
1 TSP=5 ML
1 TBSP = 15 ML
1 FL OUNCE = 30 ML
1 CUP=237 ML
1 PINT (2 CUPS) = 473 ML
1 QUART (4 CUPS)=.95 LITER
1GALLON (16 CUPS)=3.8LITERS
1 OZ=28 GRAMS
1 POUND = 454 GRAMS

BUTTER

1 CUP BUTTER=2 STICKS = 8 OUNCES = 230 GRAMS=8 TABLESPOONS

WHAT DOES 1 CUP EQUAL

1 CUP = 8 FLUID OUNCES
1 CUP = 16 TABLESPOONS
1 CUP = 48 TEASPOONS
1 CUP = 1/2 PINT
1 CUP = 1/4 QUART
1 CUP = 1/16 GALLON
1 CUP = 240 ML

BAKING PAN CONVERSIONS

1 CUP ALL-PURPOSE FLOUR=4.5 OZ
1 CUP ROLLED OATS = 3 OZ 1 LARGE EGG = 1.7 OZ
1 CUP BUTTER=8OZ 1 CUP MILK = 8 OZ
1 CUP HEAVY CREAM = 8.4 OZ
1 CUP GRANULATED SUGAR=7.1 OZ
1 CUP PACKED BROWN SUGAR = 7.75 OZ
1 CUP VEGETABLE OIL = 7.7 OZ
1 CUP UNSIFTED POWDERED SUGAR = 4.4 OZ

BAKING PAN CONVERSIONS

9-INCH ROUND CAKE PAN= 12 CUPS
10-INCH TUBE PAN =16 CUPS
11-INCH BUNDT PAN = 12 CUPS
9-INCH SPRINGFORM PAN = 10 CUPS
9 X 5 INCH LOAF PAN=8 CUPS
9-INCH SQUARE PAN=8 CUPS

Breakfast Recipes

Breakfast Stuffed Peppers

Servings: 4
Cooking Time: 13 Minutes

Ingredients:
- 2 capsicums, halved, seeds removed
- 4 eggs
- 1 teaspoon olive oil
- 1 pinch salt and pepper
- 1 pinch sriracha flakes

Directions:
1. Cut each capsicum in half and place two halves in each air fryer basket.
2. Crack one egg into each capsicum and top it with black pepper, salt, sriracha flakes and olive oil.
3. Return the air fryer basket 1 to Zone 1, and basket 2 to Zone 2 of the Ninja Foodi 2-Basket Air Fryer.
4. Choose the "Air Fry" mode for Zone 1 at 390 degrees F and 13 minutes of cooking time.
5. Select the "MATCH COOK" option to copy the settings for Zone 2.
6. Initiate cooking by pressing the START/PAUSE BUTTON.
7. Serve warm.

Nutrition:
- (Per serving) Calories 237 | Fat 19g | Sodium 518mg | Carbs 7g | Fiber 1.5g | Sugar 3.4g | Protein 12g

Yellow Potatoes With Eggs

Servings: 2
Cooking Time: 35

Ingredients:
- 1 pound of Dutch yellow potatoes, quartered
- 1 red bell pepper, chopped
- Salt and black pepper, to taste
- 1 green bell pepper, chopped
- 2 teaspoons of olive oil
- 2 teaspoons of garlic powder
- 1 teaspoon of onion powder
- 1 egg
- ¼ teaspoon of butter

Directions:
1. Toss together diced potatoes, green pepper, red pepper, salt, black pepper, and olive oil along with garlic powder and onion powder.
2. Put in the zone 1 basket of the air fryer.
3. Take ramekin and grease it with oil spray.
4. Whisk egg in a bowl and add salt and pepper along with ½ teaspoon of butter.
5. Pour egg into a ramekin and place it in a zone 2 basket.
6. Now start cooking and set a timer for zone 1 basket to 30-35 minutes at 400 degrees at AIR FRY mode.
7. Now for zone 2, set it on AIR FRY mode at 350 degrees F for 8-10 minutes.
8. Press the Smart finish button and press start, it will finish both at the same time.
9. Once done, serve and enjoy.

Nutrition:
- (Per serving) Calories 252 | Fat 7.5g | Sodium 37mg | Carbs 40g | Fiber 3.9g | Sugar 7g | Protein 6.7g

Bacon Cinnamon Rolls

Servings: 8
Cooking Time: 10 Minutes

Ingredients:
- 8 bacon strips
- 180ml bourbon
- 1 tube (310g) refrigerated cinnamon rolls with icing
- 55g chopped pecans
- 2 tablespoons maple syrup

Directions:
1. In a small bowl, combine the bacon and the bourbon. Refrigerate overnight after sealing. Remove the bacon and pat it dry; toss out the bourbon.
2. Cook bacon in batches in a large frying pan over medium heat until nearly crisp but still flexible. Remove to a plate lined with paper towels to drain.
3. Separate the dough into 8 rolls and set aside the frosting packet. Spiral rolls should be unrolled into long strips.
4. Place 1 bacon strip on each dough strip, cut as necessary, and reroll to form a spiral. To seal the ends, pinch them together.
5. Press your chosen zone - "Zone 1" or "Zone 2" and then rotate the knob to select "Air Fry".
6. Set the temperature to 175 degrees C, and then set the time for 5 minutes to preheat.
7. After preheating, spray the Air-Fryer basket of each zone with cooking spray, line them with parchment paper, and place rolls.
8. Slide the basket into the Air Fryer and set the time for 5 minutes.
9. Turn the rolls over and cook for another 4 minutes, or until golden brown.
10. Meanwhile, combine the pecans and maple syrup in a mixing bowl. In a separate bowl, combine the contents of the icing packet.
11. Heat the remaining bacon drippings in the same frying pan over medium heat. Cook, stirring regularly until the pecan mixture is gently browned, about 2-3 minutes.
12. After cooking time is completed, transfer them onto serving plates and drizzle half the icing over warm cinnamon rolls; top with half the pecans.

Sweet Potato Hash

Servings: 4
Cooking Time: 15 Minutes

Ingredients:
- 3 sweet potatoes, peel & cut into ½-inch pieces
- ½ tsp cinnamon
- 2 tbsp olive oil
- 1 bell pepper, cut into ½-inch pieces
- ½ tsp dried thyme
- ½ tsp nutmeg
- 1 medium onion, cut into ½-inch pieces
- Pepper
- Salt

Directions:
1. In a bowl, toss sweet potatoes with the remaining ingredients.
2. Insert a crisper plate in Ninja Foodi air fryer baskets.
3. Add potato mixture in both baskets.
4. Select zone 1 then select "air fry" mode and set the temperature to 355 degrees F for 15 minutes. Press "match" to match zone 2 settings to zone 1. Press "start/stop" to begin.

Nutrition:
- (Per serving) Calories 167 | Fat 7.3g | Sodium 94mg | Carbs 24.9g | Fiber 4.2g | Sugar 6.8g | Protein 2.2g

Cheesy Baked Eggs

Servings: 4
Cooking Time: 16 Minutes

Ingredients:

- 4 large eggs
- 57g smoked gouda, shredded
- Everything bagel seasoning, to taste
- Salt and pepper to taste

Directions:

1. Crack one egg in each ramekin.
2. Top the egg with bagel seasoning, black pepper, salt and gouda.
3. Place 2 ramekins in each air fryer basket.
4. Return the air fryer basket 1 to Zone 1, and basket 2 to Zone 2 of the Ninja Foodi 2-Basket Air Fryer.
5. Choose the "Air Fry" mode for Zone 1 and set the temperature to 400 degrees F and 16 minutes of cooking time.
6. Select the "MATCH COOK" option to copy the settings for Zone 2.
7. Initiate cooking by pressing the START/PAUSE BUTTON.
8. Serve warm.

Nutrition:

- (Per serving) Calories 190 | Fat 18g | Sodium 150mg | Carbs 0.6g | Fiber 0.4g | Sugar 0.4g | Protein 7.2g

Sausage With Eggs

Servings: 2
Cooking Time: 13

Ingredients:

- 4 sausage links, raw and uncooked
- 4 eggs, uncooked
- 1 tablespoon of green onion
- 2 tablespoons of chopped tomatoes
- Salt and black pepper, to taste
- 2 tablespoons of milk, dairy
- Oil spray, for greasing

Directions:

1. Take a bowl and whisk eggs in it.
2. Then pour milk, and add onions and tomatoes.
3. Whisk it all well.
4. Now season it with salt and black pepper.
5. Take one cake pan, that fit inside the air fryer and grease it with oil spray.
6. Pour the omelet in the greased cake pans.
7. Put the cake pan inside zone 1 air fryer basket of Ninja Foodie 2-Basket Air Fryer.
8. Now place the sausage link into the zone 2 basket.
9. Select bake for zone 1 basket and set the timer to 8-10 minutes at 300 degrees F.
10. For the zone 2 basket, select the AIR FRY button and set the timer to 12 minutes at 390 degrees.
11. Once the cooking cycle completes, serve by transferring it to plates.
12. Chop the sausage or cut it in round and then mix it with omelet.
13. Enjoy hot as a delicious breakfast.

Nutrition:

- (Per serving) Calories 240 | Fat 18.4g | Sodium 396mg | Carbs 2.8g | Fiber 0.2g | Sugar 2g | Protein 15.6g

Homemade Toaster Pastries

Servings: 6 Pastries
Cooking Time: 11 Minutes
Ingredients:
- Oil, for spraying
- 1 (425 g) package refrigerated piecrust
- 6 tablespoons jam or preserves of choice
- 475 ml icing sugar
- 3 tablespoons milk
- 1 to 2 tablespoons sprinkles of choice

Directions:
1. Preheat the air fryer to 176°C. Line the zone 1 air fryer drawer with parchment and spray lightly with oil.
2. Cut the piecrust into 12 rectangles, about 3 by 4 inches each. You will need to reroll the dough scraps to get 12 rectangles.
3. Spread 1 tablespoon of jam in the center of 6 rectangles, leaving ¼ inch around the edges.
4. Pour some water into a small bowl. Use your finger to moisten the edge of each rectangle.
5. Top each rectangle with another and use your fingers to press around the edges. Using the tines of a fork, seal the edges of the dough and poke a few holes in the top of each one. Place the pastries in the prepared drawer.
6. Air fry for 11 minutes. Let cool completely.
7. In a medium bowl, whisk together the icing sugar and milk. Spread the icing over the tops of the pastries and add sprinkles. Serve immediately.

Brussels Sprouts Potato Hash

Servings: 4
Cooking Time: 10 Minutes
Ingredients:
- 455g Brussels sprouts
- 1 small to medium red onion
- 227g baby red potatoes
- 2 tablespoons avocado oil
- ½ teaspoon salt
- ½ teaspoon black pepper

Directions:
1. Peel and boil potatoes in salted water for 15 minutes until soft.
2. Drain and allow them to cool down then dice.
3. Shred Brussels sprouts and toss them with potatoes and the rest of the ingredients.
4. Divide this veggies hash mixture in both of the air fryer baskets.
5. Return the air fryer basket 1 to Zone 1, and basket 2 to Zone 2 of the Ninja Foodi 2-Basket Air Fryer.
6. Choose the "Air Fry" mode for Zone 1 with 375 degrees F temperature and 10 minutes of cooking time.
7. Select the "MATCH COOK" option to copy the settings for Zone 2.
8. Initiate cooking by pressing the START/PAUSE BUTTON.
9. Shake the veggies once cooked halfway through.
10. Serve warm.

Nutrition:
- (Per serving) Calories 305 | Fat 25g | Sodium 532mg | Carbs 2.3g | Fiber 0.4g | Sugar 2g | Protein 18.3g

Cajun Breakfast Sausage

Servings: 8
Cooking Time: 15 To 20 Minutes

Ingredients:

- 680 g 85% lean turkey mince
- 3 cloves garlic, finely chopped
- ¼ onion, grated
- 1 teaspoon Tabasco sauce
- 1 teaspoon Cajun seasoning
- 1 teaspoon dried thyme
- ½ teaspoon paprika
- ½ teaspoon cayenne

Directions:

1. Preheat the air fryer to 188°C.
2. In a large bowl, combine the turkey, garlic, onion, Tabasco, Cajun seasoning, thyme, paprika, and cayenne. Mix with clean hands until thoroughly combined. Shape into 16 patties, about ½ inch thick.
3. Arrange the patties in a single layer in the two air fryer drawers. Pausing halfway through the cooking time to flip the patties, air fry for 15 to 20 minutes until a thermometer inserted into the thickest portion registers 74°C.

Double-dipped Mini Cinnamon Biscuits

Servings: 8 Biscuits
Cooking Time: 13 Minutes

Ingredients:

- 475 ml blanched almond flour
- 120 ml liquid or powdered sweetener
- 1 teaspoon baking powder
- ½ teaspoon fine sea salt
- 60 ml plus 2 tablespoons (¾ stick) very cold unsalted butter
- 60 ml unsweetened, unflavoured almond milk
- 1 large egg
- 1 teaspoon vanilla extract
- 3 teaspoons ground cinnamon
- Glaze:
- 120 ml powdered sweetener
- 60 ml double cream or unsweetened, unflavoured almond milk

Directions:

1. Preheat the air fryer to 175°C. Line a pie pan that fits into your air fryer with parchment paper. 2. In a medium-sized bowl, mix together the almond flour, sweetener , baking powder, and salt. Cut the butter into ½-inch squares, then use a hand mixer to work the butter into the dry ingredients. When you are done, the mixture should still have chunks of butter. 3. In a small bowl, whisk together the almond milk, egg, and vanilla extract until blended. Using a fork, stir the wet ingredients into the dry ingredients until large clumps form. Add the cinnamon and use your hands to swirl it into the dough. 4. Form the dough into sixteen 1-inch balls and place them on the prepared pan, spacing them about ½ inch apart. Bake in the zone 1 air fryer basket until golden, 10 to 13 minutes. Remove from the air fryer and let cool on the pan for at least 5 minutes. 5. While the biscuits bake, make the glaze: Place the powdered sweetener in a small bowl and slowly stir in the heavy cream with a fork. 6. When the biscuits have cooled somewhat, dip the tops into the glaze, allow it to dry a bit, and then dip again for a thick glaze. 7. Serve warm or at room temperature. Store unglazed biscuits in an airtight container in the refrigerator for up to 3 days or in the freezer for up to a month. Reheat in a preheated 175°C air fryer for 5 minutes, or until warmed through, and dip in the glaze as instructed above.

Quick And Easy Blueberry Muffins

Servings: 8 Muffins
Cooking Time: 12 Minutes
Ingredients:
- 315 ml flour
- 120 ml sugar
- 2 teaspoons baking powder
- ¼ teaspoon salt
- 80 ml rapeseed oil
- 1 egg
- 120 ml milk
- 160 ml blueberries, fresh or frozen and thawed

Directions:
1. Preheat the air fryer to 165ºC.
2. In a medium bowl, stir together flour, sugar, baking powder, and salt.
3. In a separate bowl, combine oil, egg, and milk and mix well.
4. Add egg mixture to dry ingredients and stir just until moistened.
5. Gently stir in the blueberries.
6. Spoon batter evenly into parchment paper-lined muffin cups.
7. Put the muffin cups in the two air fryer baskets and bake for 12 minutes or until tops spring back when touched lightly.
8. Serve immediately.

Broccoli-mushroom Frittata And Chimichanga Breakfast Burrito

Servings: 4
Cooking Time: 20 Minutes
Ingredients:
- Broccoli-Mushroom Frittata:
- 1 tablespoon olive oil
- 350 ml broccoli florets, finely chopped
- 120 ml sliced brown mushrooms
- 60 ml finely chopped onion
- ½ teaspoon salt
- ¼ teaspoon freshly ground black pepper
- 6 eggs
- 60 ml Parmesan cheese
- Chimichanga Breakfast Burrito:
- 2 large (10- to 12-inch) flour tortillas
- 120 ml canned refried beans (pinto or black work equally well)
- 4 large eggs, cooked scrambled
- 4 corn tortilla chips, crushed
- 120 ml grated chili cheese
- 12 pickled jalapeño slices
- 1 tablespoon vegetable oil
- Guacamole, salsa, and sour cream, for serving (optional)

Directions:
1. Make the Broccoli-Mushroom Frittata :

2. In a nonstick cake pan, combine the olive oil, broccoli, mushrooms, onion, salt, and pepper. Stir until the vegetables are thoroughly coated with oil. Place the cake pan in the zone 1 air fryer basket and set the air fryer to 205°C. Air fry for 5 minutes until the vegetables soften.
3. Meanwhile, in a medium bowl, whisk the eggs and Parmesan until thoroughly combined. Pour the egg mixture into the pan and shake gently to distribute the vegetables. Air fry for another 15 minutes until the eggs are set.
4. Remove from the air fryer and let sit for 5 minutes to cool slightly. Use a silicone spatula to gently lift the frittata onto a plate before serving.
5. Make the Chimichanga Breakfast Burrito :
6. Place the tortillas on a work surface and divide the refried beans between them, spreading them in a rough rectangle in the center of the tortillas. Top the beans with the scrambled eggs, crushed chips, cheese, and jalapeños. Fold one side over the fillings, then fold in each short side and roll up the rest of the way like a burrito.
7. Brush the outside of the burritos with the oil, then transfer to the zone 2 air fryer basket, seam-side down. Air fry at 175°C until the tortillas are browned and crisp and the filling is warm throughout, about 10 minutes.
8. Transfer the chimichangas to plates and serve warm with guacamole, salsa, and sour cream, if you like.

Bacon-and-eggs Avocado And Simple Scotch Eggs

Servings: 5
Cooking Time: 25 Minutes
Ingredients:
- Bacon-and-Eggs Avocado:
- 1 large egg
- 1 avocado, halved, peeled, and pitted
- 2 slices bacon
- Fresh parsley, for serving (optional)
- Sea salt flakes, for garnish (optional)
- Simple Scotch Eggs:
- 4 large hard boiled eggs
- 1 (340 g) package pork sausage meat
- 8 slices thick-cut bacon
- 4 wooden toothpicks, soaked in water for at least 30 minutes

Directions:
1. Make the Bacon-and-Eggs Avocado :
2. 1. Spray the zone 1 air fryer basket with avocado oil. Preheat the air fryer to 160°C. Fill a small bowl with cool water. Soft-boil the egg: Place the egg in the zone 1 air fryer basket. Air fry for 6 minutes for a soft yolk or 7 minutes for a cooked yolk. Transfer the egg to the bowl of cool water and let sit for 2 minutes. Peel and set aside. 3. Use a spoon to carve out extra space in the center of the avocado halves until the cavities are big enough to fit the soft-boiled egg. Place the soft-boiled egg in the center of one half of the avocado and replace the other half of the avocado on top, so the avocado appears whole on the outside. 4. Starting at one end of the avocado, wrap the bacon around the avocado to completely cover it. Use toothpicks to hold the bacon in place. 5. Place the bacon-wrapped avocado in the zone 1 air fryer basket and air fry for 5 minutes. Flip the avocado over and air fry for another 5 minutes, or until the bacon is cooked to your liking. Serve on a bed of fresh parsley, if desired, and sprinkle with salt flakes, if desired. 6. Best served fresh. Store extras in an airtight container in the fridge for up to 4 days. Reheat in a preheated 160°C air fryer for 4 minutes, or until heated through.
3. Make the Simple Scotch Eggs :
4. Slice the sausage meat into four parts and place each part into a large circle.
5. Put an egg into each circle and wrap it in the sausage. Put in the refrigerator for 1 hour.
6. Preheat the air fryer to 235°C.
7. Make a cross with two pieces of thick-cut bacon. Put a wrapped egg in the center, fold the bacon over top of the egg, and secure with a toothpick.
8. Air fry in the preheated zone 2 air fryer basket for 25 minutes.

Puff Pastry

Servings: 6
Cooking Time: 10 Minutes
Ingredients:
- 1 package (200g) cream cheese, softened
- 50g sugar
- 2 tablespoons plain flour
- ½ teaspoon vanilla extract
- 2 large egg yolks
- 1 tablespoon water
- 1 package frozen puff pastry, thawed
- 210g seedless raspberry jam

Directions:
1. Mix the cream cheese, sugar, flour, and vanilla extract until smooth, then add 1 egg yolk.
2. Combine the remaining egg yolk with the water. Unfold each sheet of puff pastry on a lightly floured board and roll into a 30 cm square. Cut into nine 10 cm squares.
3. Put 1 tablespoon cream cheese mixture and 1 rounded teaspoon jam on each. Bring 2 opposite corners of pastry over filling, sealing with yolk mixture.
4. Brush the remaining yolk mixture over the tops.
5. Press your chosen zone - "Zone 1" or "Zone 2" and then rotate the knob to select "Air Fry".
6. Set the temperature to 160 degrees C, and then set the time for 5 minutes to preheat.
7. After preheating, spray the Air-Fryer basket of each zone with cooking spray, line them with parchment paper, and place the pastry on them.
8. Slide the basket into the Air Fryer and set the time for 10 minutes.
9. After cooking time is completed, transfer them onto serving plates and serve.

Spinach And Swiss Frittata With Mushrooms

Servings: 4
Cooking Time: 20 Minutes
Ingredients:
- Olive oil cooking spray
- 8 large eggs
- ½ teaspoon salt
- ½ teaspoon black pepper
- 1 garlic clove, minced
- 475 ml fresh baby spinach
- 110 g baby mushrooms, sliced
- 1 shallot, diced
- 120 ml shredded Swiss cheese, divided
- Hot sauce, for serving (optional)

Directions:
1. Lightly coat the inside of a 6-inch round cake pan with olive oil cooking spray. In a large bowl, beat the eggs, salt, pepper, and garlic for 1 to 2 minutes, or until well combined.
2. Fold in the spinach, mushrooms, shallot, and 60 ml the Swiss cheese. Pour the egg mixture into the prepared cake pan, and sprinkle the remaining 60 ml Swiss over the top. Place into the zone 1 drawer.
3. Select Bake button and adjust temperature to 180ºC, set time to 18 to 20 minutes and press Start. After the end, remove from the air fryer and allow to cool for 5 minutes. Drizzle with hot sauce before serving.
4. Serve immediately.

Breakfast Sausage And Cauliflower

Servings: 4
Cooking Time: 45 Minutes
Ingredients:
- 450 g sausage meat, cooked and crumbled
- 475 ml double/whipping cream
- 1 head cauliflower, chopped
- 235 ml grated Cheddar cheese, plus more for topping
- 8 eggs, beaten
- Salt and ground black pepper, to taste

Directions:
1. Preheat the air fryer to 176°C.
2. In a large bowl, mix the sausage, cream, chopped cauliflower, cheese and eggs. Sprinkle with salt and ground black pepper.
3. Pour the mixture into a greased casserole dish. Bake in the preheated air fryer for 45 minutes or until firm.
4. Top with more Cheddar cheese and serve.

French Toast Sticks

Servings: 5
Cooking Time: 12 Minutes
Ingredients:
- 10 teaspoons sugar, divided
- 3¼ teaspoons cinnamon, divided
- 3 slices toast
- 1 egg
- 1 egg yolks
- 80ml milk
- 1 teaspoon sugar
- 1 teaspoon brown sugar
- 1 teaspoon vanilla
- ¼ teaspoon cinnamon

Directions:
1. Line either basket "Zone 1" and "Zone 2" with a greased piece of foil.
2. Press your chosen zone - "Zone 1" and "Zone 2" and then rotate the knob to select "Air Fryer".
3. Set the temperature to 175 degrees C, and then set the time for 3 minutes to preheat.
4. Three teaspoons of sugar and 3 teaspoons of cinnamon are whisked together in a shallow bowl. Set aside.
5. Cut each slice of bread in thirds.
6. Combine the eggs, egg yolks, milk, brown sugar, remaining sugar, vanilla, and remaining cinnamon in a shallow pan.
7. Blend everything until it's smooth.
8. Allow the bread to soak in the egg mixture for a few seconds. Flip over and dip the other side.
9. Coat both sides of the bread in the cinnamon-sugar mixture. Place in the basket.
10. Slide the basket into the Air Fryer and set the time for 8 minutes.
11. After cooking time is completed, transfer the bread to a serving plate and serve.

Red Pepper And Feta Frittata

Servings: 4
Cooking Time: 20 Minutes
Ingredients:
- Olive oil cooking spray
- 8 large eggs
- 1 medium red pepper, diced
- ½ teaspoon salt
- ½ teaspoon black pepper
- 1 garlic clove, minced
- 120 ml feta, divided

Directions:
1. Lightly coat the inside of a 6-inch round cake pan with olive oil cooking spray. In a large bowl, beat the eggs for 1 to 2 minutes, or until well combined.
2. Add the red pepper, salt, black pepper, and garlic to the eggs, and mix together until the red pepper is distributed throughout. Fold in 60 ml the feta cheese.
3. Pour the egg mixture into the prepared cake pan, and sprinkle the remaining 60 ml feta over the top. Place into the zone 1 drawer. Select Bake button and adjust temperature to 180°C, set time to 18 to 20 minutes and press Start.
4. Remove from the air fryer after the end and allow to cool for 5 minutes before serving.

Pork Sausage Eggs With Mustard Sauce

Servings: 8
Cooking Time: 12 Minutes
Ingredients:
- 450 g pork sausage meat
- 8 soft-boiled or hard-boiled eggs, peeled
- 1 large egg
- 2 tablespoons milk
- 235 ml crushed pork scratchings
- Smoky Mustard Sauce:
- 60 ml mayonnaise
- 2 tablespoons sour cream
- 1 tablespoon Dijon mustard
- 1 teaspoon chipotle hot sauce

Directions:
1. Divide the sausage into 8 portions. Take each portion of sausage, pat it down into a patty, and place 1 egg in the middle, gently wrapping the sausage around the egg until the egg is completely covered.
2. Repeat with the remaining eggs and sausage. In a small shallow bowl, whisk the egg and milk until frothy. In another shallow bowl, place the crushed pork scratchings. Working one at a time, dip a sausage-wrapped egg into the beaten egg and then into the pork scratchings, gently rolling to coat evenly. Repeat with the remaining sausage-wrapped eggs.
3. Put them half in zone 1, the remaining in zone 2. Lightly spray with olive oil. In zone 1 , select Air fry button, adjust temperature to 200°C, set time to 10 to 12 minutes. In zone 2, select Match Cook and press Start. Pause halfway through the baking time to turn the eggs, until the eggs are hot and the sausage is cooked through.
4. To make the sauce:
5. In a small bowl, combine the mayonnaise, sour cream, Dijon, and hot sauce. Whisk until thoroughly combined. Serve with the Scotch eggs.

Bacon Cheese Egg With Avocado And Potato Nuggets

Servings: 8
Cooking Time: 20 Minutes
Ingredients:
- Bacon Cheese Egg with Avocado:
- 6 large eggs
- 60 ml double cream
- 350 ml chopped cauliflower
- 235 ml shredded medium Cheddar cheese
- 1 medium avocado, peeled and pitted
- 8 tablespoons full-fat sour cream
- 2 spring onions, sliced on the bias
- 12 slices bacon, cooked and crumbled
- Potato Nuggets:
- 1 teaspoon extra virgin olive oil
- 1 clove garlic, minced
- 1 L kale, rinsed and chopped
- 475 ml potatoes, boiled and mashed
- 30 ml milk
- Salt and ground black pepper, to taste
- Cooking spray

Directions:
1. Make the Bacon Cheese Egg with Avocado :
2. In a medium bowl, whisk eggs and cream together. Pour into a round baking dish.
3. Add cauliflower and mix, then top with Cheddar. Place dish into the zone 1 air fryer drawer.
4. Adjust the temperature to 160°C and set the timer for 20 minutes.
5. When completely cooked, eggs will be firm and cheese will be browned. Slice into four pieces.
6. Slice avocado and divide evenly among pieces. Top each piece with 2 tablespoons sour cream, sliced spring onions, and crumbled bacon.
7. Make the Potato Nuggets :
8. Preheat the zone 2 air fryer drawer to 200°C.
9. In a skillet over medium heat, sauté the garlic in the olive oil, until it turns golden brown. Sauté with the kale for an additional 3 minutes and remove from the heat.
10. Mix the mashed potatoes, kale and garlic in a bowl. Pour in the milk and sprinkle with salt and pepper.
11. Shape the mixture into nuggets and spritz with cooking spray.
12. Put in the zone 2 air fryer drawer and air fry for 15 minutes, flip the nuggets halfway through cooking to make sure the nuggets fry evenly.
13. Serve immediately.

Easy Sausage Pizza

Servings: 4
Cooking Time: 6 Minutes
Ingredients:
- 2 tablespoons ketchup
- 1 pitta bread
- 80 ml sausage meat
- 230 g Mozzarella cheese
- 1 teaspoon garlic powder
- 1 tablespoon olive oil

Directions:
1. Preheat the air fryer to 170°C.
2. Spread the ketchup over the pitta bread.
3. Top with the sausage meat and cheese. Sprinkle with the garlic powder and olive oil.
4. Put the pizza in the zone 1 air fryer basket and bake for 6 minutes.
5. Serve warm.

Bacon And Eggs For Breakfast

Servings:1
Cooking Time:12
Ingredients:
- 4 strips of thick-sliced bacon
- 2 small eggs
- Salt and black pepper, to taste
- Oil spray for greasing ramekins

Directions:
1. Take 2 ramekins and grease them with oil spray.
2. Crack eggs in a bowl and season it salt and black pepper.
3. Divide the egg mixture between two ramekins.
4. Put the bacon slices into Ninja Foodie 2-Basket Air Fryer zone 1 basket, and ramekins in zone 2 baskets.
5. Now for zone 1 set it to AIR FRY mode at 400 degrees F for 12 minutes.
6. And for zone 2 set it 350 degrees for 8 minutes using AIR FRY mode.
7. Press the Smart finish button and press start, it will finish both at the same time.
8. Once done, serve and enjoy.

Nutrition:
- (Per serving) Calories131 | Fat 10g| Sodium 187mg | Carbs0.6 g | Fiber 0g | Sugar 0.6g | Protein 10.7

Breakfast Frittata

Servings: 4
Cooking Time: 12 Minutes
Ingredients:
- 4 eggs
- 4 tablespoons milk
- 35g cheddar cheese grated
- 50g feta crumbled
- 1 tomato, deseeded and chopped
- 15g spinach chopped
- 1 tablespoon fresh herbs, chopped
- 2 spring onion chopped
- Salt and black pepper, to taste
- ½ teaspoon olive oil

Directions:
1. Beat eggs with milk in a bowl and stir in the rest of the ingredients.
2. Grease two small-sized springform pans and line them with parchment paper.
3. Divide the egg mixture into the pans and place one in each air fryer basket.
4. Return the air fryer basket 1 to Zone 1, and basket 2 to Zone 2 of the Ninja Foodi 2-Basket Air Fryer.
5. Choose the "Air Fry" mode for Zone 1 at 350 degrees F and 12 minutes of cooking time.
6. Select the "MATCH COOK" option to copy the settings for Zone 2.
7. Initiate cooking by pressing the START/PAUSE BUTTON.
8. Serve warm.

Nutrition:
- (Per serving) Calories 273 | Fat 22g |Sodium 517mg | Carbs 3.3g | Fiber 0.2g | Sugar 1.4g | Protein 16.1g

Mushroom-and-tomato Stuffed Hash Browns

Servings: 4
Cooking Time: 20 Minutes
Ingredients:
- Olive oil cooking spray
- 1 tablespoon plus 2 teaspoons olive oil, divided
- 110 g baby mushrooms, diced
- 1 spring onion, white parts and green parts, diced
- 1 garlic clove, minced
- 475 ml shredded potatoes
- ½ teaspoon salt
- ¼ teaspoon black pepper
- 1 plum tomato, diced
- 120 ml shredded mozzarella

Directions:
1. Lightly coat the inside of a 6-inch cake pan with olive oil cooking spray. In a small skillet, heat 2 teaspoons olive oil over medium heat. Add the mushrooms, spring onion, and garlic, and cook for 4 to 5 minutes, or until they have softened and are beginning to show some color.
2. Remove from heat. Meanwhile, in a large bowl, combine the potatoes, salt, pepper, and the remaining tablespoon olive oil. Toss until all potatoes are well coated. Pour half of the potatoes into the bottom of the cake pan.
3. Top with the mushroom mixture, tomato, and mozzarella. Spread the remaining potatoes over the top. Place the cake pan into the zone 1 drawer.
4. Select Bake button and adjust temperature to 190°C, set time to 12 to 15 minutes and press Start. Until the top is golden brown, remove from the air fryer and allow to cool for 5 minutes before slicing and serving.

Donuts

Servings: 6
Cooking Time: 15 Minutes
Ingredients:
- 1 cup granulated sugar
- 2 tablespoons ground cinnamon
- 1 can refrigerated flaky buttermilk biscuits
- ¼ cup unsalted butter, melted

Directions:
1. Combine the sugar and cinnamon in a small shallow bowl and set aside.
2. Remove the biscuits from the can and put them on a chopping board, separated. Cut holes in the center of each biscuit with a 1-inch round biscuit cutter (or a similarly sized bottle cap).
3. Place a crisper plate in each drawer. In each drawer, place 4 biscuits in a single layer. Insert the drawers into the unit.
4. Select zone 1, then AIR FRY, then set the temperature to 360 degrees F/ 180 degrees C with a 10-minute timer. To match zone 2 settings to zone 1, choose MATCH. To begin cooking, select START/STOP.
5. Remove the donuts from the drawers after the timer has finished.

Nutrition:
- (Per serving) Calories 223 | Fat 8g | Sodium 150mg | Carbs 40g | Fiber 1.4g | Sugar 34.2g | Protein 0.8g

Onion Omelette And Buffalo Egg Cups

Servings: 4
Cooking Time: 15 Minutes
Ingredients:
- Onion Omelette:
- 3 eggs
- Salt and ground black pepper, to taste
- ½ teaspoons soy sauce
- 1 large onion, chopped
- 2 tablespoons grated Cheddar cheese
- Cooking spray
- Buffalo Egg Cups:
- 4 large eggs
- 60 g full-fat cream cheese
- 2 tablespoons buffalo sauce
- 120 ml shredded sharp Cheddar cheese

Directions:
1. Make the Onion Omelette :
2. Preheat the zone 1 air fryer drawer to 180°C.
3. In a bowl, whisk together the eggs, salt, pepper, and soy sauce.
4. Spritz a small pan with cooking spray. Spread the chopped onion across the bottom of the pan, then transfer the pan to the zone 1 air fryer drawer.
5. Bake in the preheated air fryer for 6 minutes or until the onion is translucent.
6. Add the egg mixture on top of the onions to coat well. Add the cheese on top, then continue baking for another 6 minutes.
7. Allow to cool before serving.
8. Make the Buffalo Egg Cups :
9. Crack eggs into two ramekins.
10. In a small microwave-safe bowl, mix cream cheese, buffalo sauce, and Cheddar. Microwave for 20 seconds and then stir. Place a spoonful into each ramekin on top of the eggs.
11. Place ramekins into the zone 2 air fryer drawer.
12. Adjust the temperature to 160°C and bake for 15 minutes.
13. Serve warm.

Sausage And Egg Breakfast Burrito

Servings: 6
Cooking Time: 30 Minutes
Ingredients:
- 6 eggs
- Salt and pepper, to taste
- Cooking oil
- 120 ml chopped red pepper
- 120 ml chopped green pepper
- 230 g chicken sausage meat (removed from casings)
- 120 ml salsa
- 6 medium (8-inch) flour tortillas
- 120 ml shredded Cheddar cheese

Directions:
1. In a medium bowl, whisk the eggs. Add salt and pepper to taste.

2. Place a skillet on medium-high heat. Spray with cooking oil. Add the eggs. Scramble for 2 to 3 minutes, until the eggs are fluffy. Remove the eggs from the skillet and set aside.
3. If needed, spray the skillet with more oil. Add the chopped red and green bell peppers. Cook for 2 to 3 minutes, until the peppers are soft.
4. Add the sausage meat to the skillet. Break the sausage into smaller pieces using a spatula or spoon. Cook for 3 to 4 minutes, until the sausage is brown.
5. Add the salsa and scrambled eggs. Stir to combine. Remove the skillet from heat.
6. Spoon the mixture evenly onto the tortillas.
7. To form the burritos, fold the sides of each tortilla in toward the middle and then roll up from the bottom. You can secure each burrito with a toothpick. Or you can moisten the outside edge of the tortilla with a small amount of water. I prefer to use a cooking brush, but you can also dab with your fingers.
8. Spray the burritos with cooking oil and place them in the two air fryer drawers. Do not stack. Air fry at 204°C for 8 minutes.
9. Open the air fryer and flip the burritos. Cook for an additional 2 minutes or until crisp.
10. Sprinkle the Cheddar cheese over the burritos. Cool before serving.

Sweet Potato Sausage Hash

Servings: 4
Cooking Time: 20 Minutes
Ingredients:
- 1½ pounds sweet potato, peeled and diced into ½-inch pieces
- 1 tablespoon minced garlic
- 1 teaspoon kosher salt plus more, as desired
- Ground black pepper, as desired
- 2 tablespoons canola oil
- 1 tablespoon dried sage
- 1-pound uncooked mild ground breakfast sausage
- ½ large onion, peeled and diced
- ½ teaspoon ground cinnamon
- 1 teaspoon chili powder
- 4 large eggs, poached or fried (optional)

Directions:
1. Toss the sweet potatoes with the garlic, salt, pepper, and canola oil in a mixing bowl.
2. Install the crisper plate in the zone 1 drawer, fill it with the sweet potato mixture, and insert the drawer in the unit.
3. Place the ground sausage in the zone 2 drawer (without the crisper plate) and place it in the unit.
4. Select zone 1, then AIR FRY, and set the temperature to 400 degrees F/ 200 degrees C with a 30-minute timer.
5. Select zone 2, then ROAST, then set the temperature to 400 degrees F/ 200 degrees C with a 20-minute timer. SYNC is the option to choose. To begin cooking, press the START/STOP button.
6. When the zone 1 and zone 2 times have reached 10 minutes, press START/STOP and remove the drawers from the unit. Shake each for 10 seconds.
7. Half of the sage should be added to the zone 1 drawer.
8. Add the onion to the zone 2 drawer and mix to incorporate. To continue cooking, press START/STOP and reinsert the drawers.
9. Remove both drawers from the unit once the cooking is finished and add the potatoes to the sausage mixture. Mix in the cinnamon, sage, chili powder, and salt until thoroughly combined.
10. When the hash is done, stir it and serve it right away with a poached or fried egg on top, if desired.

Nutrition:
- (Per serving) Calories 491 | Fat 19.5g | Sodium 736mg | Carbs 51g | Fiber 8g | Sugar 2g | Protein 26.3

Wholemeal Banana-walnut Bread

Servings: 6
Cooking Time: 23 Minutes
Ingredients:
- Olive oil cooking spray
- 2 ripe medium bananas
- 1 large egg
- 60 ml non-fat plain Greek yoghurt
- 60 ml olive oil
- ½ teaspoon vanilla extract
- 2 tablespoons honey
- 235 ml wholemeal flour
- ¼ teaspoon salt
- ¼ teaspoon baking soda
- ½ teaspoon ground cinnamon
- 60 ml chopped walnuts

Directions:
1. Lightly coat the inside of two 5 ½-by-3-inch loaf pans with olive oil cooking spray.
2. In a large bowl, mash the bananas with a fork. Add the egg, yoghurt, olive oil, vanilla, and honey. Mix until well combined and mostly smooth. Sift the wholemeal flour, salt, baking soda, and cinnamon into the wet mixture, then stir until just combined. Do not overmix. Gently fold in the walnuts. Pour into the prepared loaf pans and spread to distribute evenly.
3. Place a loaf pan in the zone 1 drawer and another pan into zone 2 drawer. In zone 1, select Bake button and adjust temperature to 180°C, set time to 20 to 23 minutes. In zone 2, select Match Cook and press Start.
4. Remove until golden brown on top and a toothpick inserted into the center comes out clean. Allow to cool for 5 minutes before serving.

Fish And Seafood Recipes

Easy Herbed Salmon

Servings: 2
Cooking Time: 5 Minutes
Ingredients:
- 2 salmon fillets
- 1 tbsp butter
- 2 tbsp olive oil
- 1/4 tsp paprika
- 1 tsp herb de Provence
- Pepper
- Salt

Directions:
1. Brush salmon fillets with oil and sprinkle with paprika, herb de Provence, pepper, and salt.
2. Place salmon fillets into the air fryer basket and cook at 390 F for 5 minutes.
3. Melt butter in a pan and pour over cooked salmon fillets.
4. Serve and enjoy.

Crispy Parmesan Cod

Servings: 2
Cooking Time: 10 Minutes
Ingredients:
- 455g cod filets
- Salt and black pepper, to taste
- ½ cup flour
- 2 large eggs, beaten
- ½ teaspoon salt
- 1 cup Panko
- ½ cup grated parmesan
- 2 teaspoons old bay seasoning
- ½ teaspoon garlic powder
- Olive oil spray

Directions:
1. Rub the cod fillets with black pepper and salt.
2. Mix panko with parmesan cheese, old bay seasoning, and garlic powder in a bowl.
3. Mix flour with salt in another bowl.
4. Dredge the cod filets in the flour then dip in the eggs and coat with the Panko mixture.
5. Place the cod fillets in the air fryer baskets.
6. Return the air fryer basket 1 to Zone 1, and basket 2 to Zone 2 of the Ninja Foodi 2-Basket Air Fryer.
7. Choose the "Air Fry" mode for Zone 1 and set the temperature to 400 degrees F and 10 minutes of cooking time.
8. Select the "MATCH COOK" option to copy the settings for Zone 2.
9. Initiate cooking by pressing the START/PAUSE BUTTON.
10. Flip the cod fillets once cooked halfway through.
11. Serve warm.

Nutrition:
- (Per serving) Calories 275 | Fat 1.4g | Sodium 582mg | Carbs 31.5g | Fiber 1.1g | Sugar 0.1g | Protein 29.8g

Herb Lemon Mussels

Servings: 6
Cooking Time: 10 Minutes
Ingredients:
- 1kg mussels, steamed & half shell
- 1 tbsp thyme, chopped
- 1 tbsp parsley, chopped
- 1 tsp dried parsley
- 1 tsp garlic, minced
- 60ml olive oil
- 45ml lemon juice
- Pepper
- Salt

Directions:
1. In a bowl, mix mussels with the remaining ingredients.
2. Insert a crisper plate in the Ninja Foodi air fryer baskets.
3. Add the mussels to both baskets.
4. Select zone 1 then select "air fry" mode and set the temperature to 360 degrees F for 10 minutes. Press "match" to match zone 2 settings to zone 1. Press "start/stop" to begin.

Nutrition:
- (Per serving) Calories 206 | Fat 11.9g | Sodium 462mg | Carbs 6.3g | Fiber 0.3g | Sugar 0.2g | Protein 18.2g

Rainbow Salmon Kebabs And Tuna Melt

Servings: 3
Cooking Time: 10 Minutes
Ingredients:
- Rainbow Salmon Kebabs:
- 170 g boneless, skinless salmon, cut into 1-inch cubes
- ¼ medium red onion, peeled and cut into 1-inch pieces
- ½ medium yellow bell pepper, seeded and cut into 1-inch pieces
- ½ medium courgette, trimmed and cut into ½-inch slices
- 1 tablespoon olive oil
- ½ teaspoon salt
- ¼ teaspoon ground black pepper
- Tuna Melt:
- Olive or vegetable oil, for spraying
- 140 g can tuna, drained
- 1 tablespoon mayonnaise
- ¼ teaspoon garlic granules, plus more for garnish
- 2 teaspoons unsalted butte
- 2 slices sandwich bread of choice
- 2 slices Cheddar cheese

Directions:
1. Make the Rainbow Salmon Kebabs : Using one skewer, skewer 1 piece salmon, then 1 piece onion, 1 piece bell pepper, and finally 1 piece courgette. Repeat this pattern with additional skewers to make four kebabs total. Drizzle with olive oil and sprinkle with salt and black pepper. 2. Place kebabs into the ungreased zone 1 air fryer drawer. Adjust the temperature to 204°C and air fry for 8 minutes, turning kebabs halfway through cooking. Salmon will easily flake and have an internal temperature of at least 64°C when done; vegetables will be tender. Serve warm.
2. Make the Tuna Melt : 1. Line the zone 2 air fryer drawer with baking paper and spray lightly with oil. In a medium bowl, mix together the tuna, mayonnaise, and garlic. 3. Spread 1 teaspoon of butter on each slice of bread and place one slice butter-side down in the prepared drawer. 4. Top with a slice of cheese, the tuna mixture, another slice of cheese, and the other slice of bread, butter-side up. 5. Air fry at 204°C for 5 minutes, flip, and cook for another 5 minutes, until browned and crispy. 6. Sprinkle with additional garlic, before cutting in half and serving.

Dukkah-crusted Halibut

Servings: 2
Cooking Time: 17 Minutes
Ingredients:
- Dukkah:
- 1 tablespoon coriander seeds
- 1 tablespoon sesame seeds
- 1½ teaspoons cumin seeds
- 50 g roasted mixed nuts
- ¼ teaspoon kosher or coarse sea salt
- ¼ teaspoon black pepper
- Fish:
- 2 halibut fillets, 140 g each
- 2 tablespoons mayonnaise
- Vegetable oil spray

- Lemon wedges, for serving

Directions:
1. For the Dukkah: Combine the coriander, sesame seeds, and cumin in a small baking pan. Place the pan in the zone 1 air fryer basket. Set the air fryer to 205°C for 5 minutes. Toward the end of the cooking time, you will hear the seeds popping. Transfer to a plate and let cool for 5 minutes. 2. Transfer the toasted seeds to a food processor or spice grinder and add the mixed nuts. Pulse until coarsely chopped. Add the salt and pepper and stir well.
2. 3. For the fish: Spread each fillet with 1 tablespoon of the mayonnaise. Press a heaping tablespoon of the Dukkah into the mayonnaise on each fillet, pressing lightly to adhere. 4. Spray the zone 2 air fryer basket with vegetable oil spray. Place the fish in the zone 2 basket. Cook for 12 minutes, or until the fish flakes easily with a fork. 5. Serve the fish with lemon wedges.

"fried" Fish With Seasoned Potato Wedges

Servings:4
Cooking Time: 30 Minutes

Ingredients:
- FOR THE FISH
- 4 cod fillets (6 ounces each)
- 4 tablespoons all-purpose flour, divided
- ¼ cup cornstarch
- 1 teaspoon baking powder
- ¼ teaspoon kosher salt
- ⅓ cup lager-style beer or sparkling water
- Tartar sauce, cocktail sauce, or malt vinegar, for serving (optional)
- FOR THE POTATOES
- 4 russet potatoes
- 2 tablespoons vegetable oil
- ½ teaspoon paprika
- ½ teaspoon kosher salt
- ¼ teaspoon garlic powder
- ¼ teaspoon freshly ground black pepper

Directions:
1. To prep the fish: Pat the fish dry with a paper towel and coat lightly with 2 tablespoons of flour.
2. In a shallow dish, combine the remaining 2 tablespoons of flour, the cornstarch, baking powder, and salt. Stir in the beer to form a thick batter.
3. Dip the fish in the batter to coat both sides, then let rest on a cutting board for 10 minutes.
4. To prep the potatoes: Cut each potato in half lengthwise, then cut each half into 4 wedges.
5. In a large bowl, combine the potatoes and oil. Toss well to fully coat the potatoes. Add the paprika, salt, garlic powder, and black pepper and toss well to coat.
6. To cook the fish and potato wedges: Install a crisper plate in each of the two baskets. Place a piece of parchment paper or aluminum foil over the plate in the Zone 1 basket. Place the fish in the basket and insert the basket in the unit. Place the potato wedges in a single layer in the Zone 2 basket and insert the basket in the unit.
7. Select Zone 1, select AIR FRY, set the temperature to 400°F, and set the timer to 13 minutes.
8. Select Zone 2, select AIR FRY, set the temperature to 400°F, and set the timer to 30 minutes. Select SMART FINISH.
9. Press START/PAUSE to begin cooking.
10. When the Zone 1 timer reads 5 minutes, press START/PAUSE. Remove the basket and use a silicone spatula to carefully flip the fish over. Reinsert the basket and press START/PAUSE to resume cooking.
11. When cooking is complete, the fish should be cooked through and the potatoes crispy outside and tender inside. Serve hot with tartar sauce, cocktail sauce, or malt vinegar (if using).

Nutrition:
- (Per serving) Calories: 360; Total fat: 8g; Saturated fat: 1g; Carbohydrates: 40g; Fiber: 2g; Protein: 30g; Sodium: 302mg

Simple Buttery Cod & Salmon On Bed Of Fennel And Carrot

Servings: 4
Cooking Time: 13 To 14 Minutes
Ingredients:
- Simple Buttery Cod:
- 2 cod fillets, 110 g each
- 2 tablespoons salted butter, melted
- 1 teaspoon Old Bay seasoning
- ½ medium lemon, sliced
- Salmon on Bed of Fennel and Carrot:
- 1 fennel bulb, thinly sliced
- 1 large carrot, peeled and sliced
- 1 small onion, thinly sliced
- 60 ml low-fat sour cream
- ¼ teaspoon coarsely ground pepper
- 2 salmon fillets, 140 g each

Directions:
1. Make the Simple Buttery Cod :
2. Place cod fillets into a round baking dish. Brush each fillet with butter and sprinkle with Old Bay seasoning. Lay two lemon slices on each fillet. Cover the dish with foil and place into the zone 1 air fryer basket.
3. Adjust the temperature to 175°C and bake for 8 minutes. Flip halfway through the cooking time. When cooked, internal temperature should be at least 65°C. Serve warm.
4. Make the Salmon on Bed of Fennel and Carrot :
5. Combine the fennel, carrot, and onion in a bowl and toss.
6. Put the vegetable mixture into a baking pan. Roast in the zone 2 air fryer basket at 205°C for 4 minutes or until the vegetables are crisp-tender.
7. Remove the pan from the air fryer. Stir in the sour cream and sprinkle the vegetables with the pepper.
8. Top with the salmon fillets.
9. Return the pan to the air fryer. Roast for another 9 to 10 minutes or until the salmon just barely flakes when tested with a fork.

Honey Teriyaki Tilapia

Servings: 4
Cooking Time: 10 Minutes
Ingredients:
- 8 tablespoons low-sodium teriyaki sauce
- 3 tablespoons honey
- 2 garlic cloves, minced
- 2 tablespoons extra virgin olive oil
- 3 pieces tilapia (each cut into 2 pieces)

Directions:
1. Combine all the first 4 ingredients to make the marinade.
2. Pour the marinade over the tilapia and let it sit for 20 minutes.
3. Place a crisper plate in each drawer. Place the tilapia in the drawers. Insert the drawers into the unit.
4. Select zone 1, then AIR FRY, then set the temperature to 360 degrees F/ 180 degrees C with a 10-minute timer. To match zone 2 settings to zone 1, choose MATCH. To begin, select START/STOP.
5. Remove the tilapia from the drawers after the timer has finished.

Nutrition:
- (Per serving) Calories 350 | Fat 16.4g | Sodium 706mg | Carbs 19.3g | Fiber 0.1g | Sugar 19g | Protein 29.3g

Fish Sandwich

Servings: 4
Cooking Time: 22 Minutes
Ingredients:
- 4 small cod fillets, skinless
- Salt and black pepper, to taste
- 2 tablespoons flour
- ¼ cup dried breadcrumbs
- Spray oil
- 9 ounces of frozen peas
- 1 tablespoon creme fraiche
- 12 capers
- 1 squeeze of lemon juice
- 4 bread rolls, cut in halve

Directions:
1. First, coat the cod fillets with flour, salt, and black pepper.
2. Then coat the fish with breadcrumbs.
3. Divide the coated codfish in the two crisper plates and spray them with cooking spray.
4. Return the crisper plate to the Ninja Foodi Dual Zone Air Fryer.
5. Choose the Air Fry mode for Zone 1 and set the temperature to 390 degrees F and the time to 17 minutes|
6. Select the "MATCH" button to copy the settings for Zone 2.
7. Initiate cooking by pressing the START/STOP button.
8. Meanwhile, boil peas in hot water for 5 minutes until soft.
9. Then drain the peas and transfer them to the blender.
10. Add capers, lemon juice, and crème fraiche to the blender.
11. Blend until it makes a smooth mixture.
12. Spread the peas crème mixture on top of 2 lower halves of the bread roll, and place the fish fillets on it.
13. Place the remaining bread slices on top.
14. Serve fresh.

Fish Fillets With Lemon-dill Sauce

Servings: 4
Cooking Time: 7 Minutes
Ingredients:
- 455 g snapper, grouper, or salmon fillets
- Sea salt and freshly ground black pepper, to taste
- 1 tablespoon avocado oil
- 60 g sour cream
- 60 g mayonnaise
- 2 tablespoons fresh dill, chopped, plus more for garnish
- 1 tablespoon freshly squeezed lemon juice
- ½ teaspoon grated lemon zest

Directions:
1. Pat the fish dry with paper towels and season well with salt and pepper. Brush with the avocado oil. 2. Set the air fryer to 204°C. Place the fillets in the two air fryer drawers and air fry for 1 minute. 3. Lower the air fryer temperature to 164°C and continue cooking for 5 minutes. Flip the fish and cook for 1 minute more or until an instant-read thermometer reads 64°C. 4. While the fish is cooking, make the sauce by combining the sour cream, mayonnaise, dill, lemon juice, and lemon zest in a medium bowl. Season with salt and pepper and stir until combined. Refrigerate until ready to serve. 5. Serve the fish with the sauce, garnished with the remaining dill.

Tilapia With Mojo And Crispy Plantains

Servings: 4
Cooking Time: 30 Minutes

Ingredients:
- FOR THE TILAPIA
- 4 tilapia fillets (6 ounces each)
- 2 tablespoons all-purpose flour
- Nonstick cooking spray
- ¼ cup freshly squeezed orange juice
- 3 tablespoons fresh lime juice
- 2 tablespoons olive oil
- 1 tablespoon minced garlic
- ½ teaspoon ground cumin
- ¼ teaspoon kosher salt
- FOR THE PLANTAINS
- 1 large green plantain
- 2 cups cold water
- 2 teaspoons kosher salt
- Nonstick cooking spray

Directions:
1. To prep the tilapia: Dust both sides of the tilapia fillets with the flour, then spritz with cooking spray.
2. In a small bowl, whisk together the orange juice, lime juice, oil, garlic, cumin, and salt. Set the mojo sauce aside.
3. To prep the plantains: Cut the ends from the plantain, then remove and discard the peel. Slice the plantain into 1-inch rounds.
4. In a large bowl, combine the water, salt, and plantains. Let soak for 15 minutes.
5. Drain the plantains and pat them dry with paper towels. Spray with cooking spray.
6. To cook the tilapia and plantains: Install a crisper plate in each of the two baskets. Place the tilapia in a single layer in the Zone 1 basket (work in batches if needed) and insert the basket in the unit. Place the plantains in the Zone 2 basket and insert the basket in the unit.
7. Select Zone 1, select AIR FRY, set the temperature to 390°F, and set the timer to 10 minutes.
8. Select Zone 2, select AIR FRY, set the temperature to 390°F, and set the timer to 30 minutes. Select SMART FINISH.
9. Press START/PAUSE to begin cooking.
10. When the Zone 2 timer reads 10 minutes, press START/PAUSE. Remove the basket and use silicone-tipped tongs to transfer the plantains, which should be tender, to a cutting board. Use the bottom of a heavy glass to smash each plantain flat. Spray both sides with cooking spray and place them back in the basket. Reinsert the basket and press START/PAUSE to resume cooking.
11. When the Zone 1 timer reads 5 minutes, press START/PAUSE. Remove the basket. Spoon half of the mojo sauce over the tilapia. Reinsert the basket and press START/PAUSE to resume cooking.
12. When cooking is complete, the fish should be cooked through and the plantains crispy. Serve the tilapia and plantains with the remaining mojo sauce for dipping.

Nutrition:
- (Per serving) Calories: 380; Total fat: 21g; Saturated fat: 2g; Carbohydrates: 20g; Fiber: 1g; Protein: 35g; Sodium: 217mg

Keto Baked Salmon With Pesto

Servings: 2
Cooking Time: 18

Ingredients:
- 4 salmon fillets, 2 inches thick
- 2 ounces green pesto
- Salt and black pepper
- ½ tablespoon of canola oil, for greasing
- 1-1/2 cup mayonnaise
- 2 tablespoons Greek yogurt
- Salt and black pepper, to taste

Directions:
1. Rub the salmon with pesto, salt, oil, and black pepper.
2. In a small bowl, whisk together all the green sauce ingredients.
3. Divide the fish fillets between both the baskets.
4. Set zone 1 to air fry mode for 18 minutes at 390 degrees F.
5. Select MATCH button for Zone 2 basket.
6. Once the cooking is done, serve it with green sauce drizzle.
7. Enjoy.

Nutrition:
- (Per serving) Calories 1165 | Fat 80.7 g| Sodium 1087 mg | Carbs 33.1g | Fiber 0.5g | Sugar 11.5 g | Protein 80.6g

Tandoori Prawns

Servings: 4
Cooking Time: 6 Minutes

Ingredients:
- 455 g jumbo raw prawns (21 to 25 count), peeled and deveined
- 1 tablespoon minced fresh ginger
- 3 cloves garlic, minced
- 5 g chopped fresh coriander or parsley, plus more for garnish
- 1 teaspoon ground turmeric
- 1 teaspoon garam masala
- 1 teaspoon smoked paprika
- 1 teaspoon kosher or coarse sea salt
- ½ to 1 teaspoon cayenne pepper
- 2 tablespoons olive oil (for Paleo) or melted ghee
- 2 teaspoons fresh lemon juice

Directions:
1. In a large bowl, combine the prawns, ginger, garlic, coriander, turmeric, garam masala, paprika, salt, and cayenne. Toss well to coat. Add the oil or ghee and toss again. Marinate at room temperature for 15 minutes, or cover and refrigerate for up to 8 hours.
2. Place the prawns in a single layer in the two air fryer baskets. Set the air fryer to 165°C for 6 minutes. Transfer the prawns to a serving platter. Cover and let the prawns finish cooking in the residual heat, about 5 minutes.
3. Sprinkle the prawns with the lemon juice and toss to coat. Garnish with additional cilantro and serve.

Scallops With Greens

Servings: 8
Cooking Time: 13 Minutes
Ingredients:
- ¾ cup heavy whipping cream
- 1 tablespoon tomato paste
- 1 tablespoon chopped fresh basil
- 1 teaspoon garlic, minced
- ½ teaspoons salt
- ½ teaspoons pepper
- 12 ounces frozen spinach thawed
- 8 jumbo sea scallops
- Vegetable oil to spray

Directions:
1. Season the scallops with vegetable oil, salt, and pepper in a bowl
2. Mix cream with spinach, basil, garlic, salt, pepper, and tomato paste in a bowl.
3. Pour this mixture over the scallops and mix gently.
4. Divide the scallops in the Air Fryers Baskets without using the crisper plate.
5. Return the crisper plate to the Ninja Foodi Dual Zone Air Fryer.
6. Choose the Air Fry mode for Zone 1 and set the temperature to 390 degrees F and the time to 13 minutes
7. Select the "MATCH" button to copy the settings for Zone 2.
8. Initiate cooking by pressing the START/STOP button.
9. Serve right away

Crumb-topped Sole

Servings: 4
Cooking Time: 7 Minutes
Ingredients:
- 3 tablespoons mayonnaise
- 3 tablespoons Parmesan cheese, grated
- 2 teaspoons mustard seeds
- ¼ teaspoon black pepper
- 4 (170g) sole fillets
- 1 cup soft bread crumbs
- 1 green onion, chopped
- ½ teaspoon ground mustard
- 2 teaspoons butter, melted
- Cooking spray

Directions:
1. Mix mayonnaise with black pepper, mustard seeds, and 2 tablespoons cheese in a bowl.
2. Place 2 sole fillets in each air fryer basket and top them with mayo mixture.
3. Mix breadcrumbs with rest of the ingredients in a bowl.
4. Drizzle this mixture over the sole fillets.
5. Return the air fryer basket 1 to Zone 1, and basket 2 to Zone 2 of the Ninja Foodi 2-Basket Air Fryer.
6. Choose the "Air Fry" mode for Zone 1 and set the temperature to 375 degrees F and 7 minutes of cooking time.
7. Select the "MATCH COOK" option to copy the settings for Zone 2.
8. Initiate cooking by pressing the START/PAUSE BUTTON.
9. Serve warm.

Nutrition:
- (Per serving) Calories 308 | Fat 24g | Sodium 715mg | Carbs 0.8g | Fiber 0.1g | Sugar 0.1g | Protein 21.9g

Salmon Nuggets

Servings: 4
Cooking Time: 15 Minutes
Ingredients:
- ⅓ cup maple syrup
- ¼ teaspoon dried chipotle pepper
- 1 pinch sea salt
- 1 ½ cups croutons
- 1 large egg
- 1 (1 pound) skinless salmon fillet, cut into 1 ½-inch chunk
- cooking spray

Directions:
1. Mix chipotle powder, maple syrup, and salt in a saucepan and cook on a simmer for 5 minutes
2. Crush the croutons in a food processor and transfer to a bowl.
3. Beat egg in another shallow bowl.
4. Season the salmon chunks with sea salt.
5. Dip the salmon in the egg, then coat with breadcrumbs.
6. Divide the coated salmon chunks in the two crisper plates.
7. Return the crisper plate to the Ninja Foodi Dual Zone Air Fryer.
8. Select the Air Fry mode for Zone 1 and set the temperature to 390 degrees F and the time to 10 minutes
9. Press the "MATCH" button to copy the settings for Zone 2.
10. Initiate cooking by pressing the START/STOP button.
11. Flip the chunks once cooked halfway through, then resume cooking.
12. Pour the maple syrup on top and serve warm.

Thai Prawn Skewers And Lemon-tarragon Fish En Papillote

Servings: 5
Cooking Time: 15 Minutes
Ingredients:
- Lemon-Tarragon Fish en Papillote:
- Salt and pepper, to taste
- 340 g extra-large prawns, peeled and deveined
- 1 tablespoon vegetable oil
- 1 teaspoon honey
- ½ teaspoon grated lime zest plus 1 tablespoon juice, plus lime wedges for serving
- 6 (6-inch) wooden skewers
- 3 tablespoons creamy peanut butter
- 3 tablespoons hot tap water
- 1 tablespoon chopped fresh coriander
- 1 teaspoon fish sauce
- Lemon-Tarragon Fish en Papillote:
- 2 tablespoons salted butter, melted
- 1 tablespoon fresh lemon juice
- ½ teaspoon dried tarragon, crushed, or 2 sprigs fresh tarragon
- 1 teaspoon kosher or coarse sea salt
- 85 g julienned carrots
- 435 g julienned fennel, or 1 stalk julienned celery
- 75 g thinly sliced red bell pepper
- 2 cod fillets, 170 g each, thawed if frozen

- Vegetable oil spray
- ½ teaspoon black pepper

Directions:
1. Make the Lemon-Tarragon Fish en Papillote :
2. Preheat the air fryer to 204°C.
3. Dissolve 2 tablespoons salt in 1 litre cold water in a large container. Add prawns, cover, and refrigerate for 15 minutes.
4. Remove prawns from brine and pat dry with paper towels. Whisk oil, honey, lime zest, and ¼ teaspoon pepper together in a large bowl. Add prawns and toss to coat. Thread prawns onto skewers, leaving about ¼ inch between each prawns .
5. Arrange 3 skewers in the zone 1 air fryer drawer, parallel to each other and spaced evenly apart. Arrange remaining 3 skewers on top, perpendicular to the bottom layer. Air fry until prawns are opaque throughout, 6 to 8 minutes, flipping and rotating skewers halfway through cooking.
6. Whisk peanut butter, hot tap water, lime juice, coriander, and fish sauce together in a bowl until smooth. Serve skewers with peanut dipping sauce and lime wedges.
7. Make the Lemon-Tarragon Fish en Papillote :
8. In a medium bowl, combine the butter, lemon juice, tarragon, and ½ teaspoon of the salt. Whisk well until you get a creamy sauce. Add the carrots, fennel, and bell pepper and toss to combine; set aside.
9. Cut two squares of baking paper each large enough to hold one fillet and half the vegetables. Spray the fillets with vegetable oil spray. Season both sides with the remaining ½ teaspoon salt and the black pepper.
10. Lay one fillet down on each baking paper square. Top each with half the vegetables. Pour any remaining sauce over the vegetables.
11. Fold over the baking paper and crimp the sides in small, tight folds to hold the fish, vegetables, and sauce securely inside the packet. Place the packets in the zone 2 air fryer drawer. Set the air fryer to 176°C for 15 minutes.
12. Transfer each packet to a plate. Cut open with scissors just before serving .

Air Fryer Calamari

Servings: 4
Cooking Time: 7 Minutes

Ingredients:
- ½ cup all-purpose flour
- 1 large egg
- 59ml milk
- 2 cups panko bread crumbs
- 1 teaspoon sea salt
- 1 teaspoon black pepper
- 455g calamari rings
- nonstick cooking spray

Directions:
1. Beat egg with milk in a bowl.
2. Mix flour with black pepper and salt in a bowl.
3. Coat the calamari rings with the flour mixture then dip in the egg mixture and coat with the breadcrumbs.
4. Place the coated calamari in the air fryer baskets.
5. Return the air fryer basket 1 to Zone 1, and basket 2 to Zone 2 of the Ninja Foodi 2-Basket Air Fryer.
6. Choose the "Air Fry" mode for Zone 1 at 400 degrees F and 7 minutes of cooking time.
7. Select the "MATCH COOK" option to copy the settings for Zone 2.
8. Initiate cooking by pressing the START/PAUSE BUTTON.
9. Flip the calamari rings once cooked half way through.
10. Serve warm.

Nutrition:
- (Per serving) Calories 336 | Fat 6g |Sodium 181mg | Carbs 1.3g | Fiber 0.2g | Sugar 0.4g | Protein 69.2g

Nutty Prawns With Amaretto Glaze

Servings: 10 To 12
Cooking Time: 10 Minutes

Ingredients:
- 120 g plain flour
- ½ teaspoon baking powder
- 1 teaspoon salt
- 2 eggs, beaten
- 120 ml milk
- 2 tablespoons olive or vegetable oil
- 185 g sliced almonds
- 900 g large prawns (about 32 to 40 prawns), peeled and deveined, tails left on
- 470 ml amaretto liqueur

Directions:
1. Combine the flour, baking powder and salt in a large bowl. Add the eggs, milk and oil and stir until it forms a smooth batter. Coarsely crush the sliced almonds into a second shallow dish with your hands.
2. Dry the prawns well with paper towels. Dip the prawns into the batter and shake off any excess batter, leaving just enough to lightly coat the prawns. Transfer the prawns to the dish with the almonds and coat completely. Place the coated prawns on a plate or baking sheet and when all the prawns have been coated, freeze the prawns for an 1 hour, or as long as a week before air frying.
3. Preheat the air fryer to 204°C.
4. Transfer frozen prawns to the two air fryer drawers. Air fry for 6 minutes. Turn the prawns over and air fry for an additional 4 minutes.
5. While the prawns are cooking, bring the Amaretto to a boil in a small saucepan on the stovetop. Lower the heat and simmer until it has reduced and thickened into a glaze, about 10 minutes.
6. Remove the prawns from the air fryer and brush both sides with the warm amaretto glaze. Serve warm.

Furikake Salmon

Servings: 4
Cooking Time: 10 Minutes

Ingredients:
- ½ cup mayonnaise
- 1 tablespoon shoyu
- 455g salmon fillet
- Salt and black pepper to taste
- 2 tablespoons furikake

Directions:
1. Mix shoyu with mayonnaise in a small bowl.
2. Rub the salmon with black pepper and salt.
3. Place the salmon pieces in the air fryer baskets.
4. Top them with the mayo mixture.
5. Return the air fryer basket 1 to Zone 1, and basket 2 to Zone 2 of the Ninja Foodi 2-Basket Air Fryer.
6. Choose the "Air Fry" mode for Zone 1 at 400 degrees F and 10 minutes of cooking time.
7. Select the "MATCH COOK" option to copy the settings for Zone 2.
8. Initiate cooking by pressing the START/PAUSE BUTTON.
9. Serve warm.

Nutrition:
- (Per serving) Calories 297 | Fat 1g | Sodium 291mg | Carbs 35g | Fiber 1g | Sugar 9g | Protein 29g

Prawns Curry And Paprika Crab Burgers

Servings: 7
Cooking Time: 14 Minutes

Ingredients:

- Prawns Curry:
- 180 ml unsweetened full-fat coconut milk
- 10 g finely chopped yellow onion
- 2 teaspoons garam masala
- 1 tablespoon minced fresh ginger
- 1 tablespoon minced garlic
- 1 teaspoon ground turmeric
- 1 teaspoon salt
- ¼ to ½ teaspoon cayenne pepper
- 455 g raw prawns (21 to 25 count), peeled and deveined
- 2 teaspoons chopped fresh coriander
- Paprika Crab Burgers:
- 2 eggs, beaten
- 1 shallot, chopped
- 2 garlic cloves, crushed
- 1 tablespoon olive oil
- 1 teaspoon yellow mustard
- 1 teaspoon fresh coriander, chopped
- 280 g crab meat
- 1 teaspoon smoked paprika
- ½ teaspoon ground black pepper
- Sea salt, to taste
- 70 g Parmesan cheese

Directions:

1. Make the Prawns Curry :
2. In a large bowl, stir together the coconut milk, onion, garam masala, ginger, garlic, turmeric, salt and cayenne, until well blended.
3. Add the prawns and toss until coated with sauce on all sides. Marinate at room temperature for 30 minutes.
4. Transfer the prawns and marinade to a baking pan. Place the pan in the zone 1 air fryer basket. Set the air fryer to 190°C for 10 minutes, stirring halfway through the cooking time.
5. Transfer the prawns to a serving bowl or platter. Sprinkle with the cilantro and serve.
6. Make the Paprika Crab Burgers :
7. In a mixing bowl, thoroughly combine the eggs, shallot, garlic, olive oil, mustard, coriander, crab meat, paprika, black pepper, and salt. Mix until well combined.
8. Shape the mixture into 6 patties. Roll the crab patties over grated Parmesan cheese, coating well on all sides. Place in your refrigerator for 2 hours.
9. Spritz the crab patties with cooking oil on both sides. Cook in the preheated zone 2 air fryer basket at 180°C for 14 minutes. Serve on dinner rolls if desired. Bon appétit!

Salmon Patties

Servings: 8
Cooking Time: 18 Minutes
Ingredients:
- 1 lb. fresh Atlantic salmon side
- ¼ cup avocado, mashed
- ¼ cup cilantro, diced
- 1 ½ teaspoons yellow curry powder
- ½ teaspoons sea salt
- ¼ cup, 4 teaspoons tapioca starch
- 2 brown eggs
- ½ cup coconut flakes
- Coconut oil, melted, for brushing
- For the greens:
- 2 teaspoons organic coconut oil, melted
- 6 cups arugula & spinach mix, tightly packed
- Pinch of sea salt

Directions:
1. Remove the fish skin and dice the flesh.
2. Place in a large bowl. Add cilantro, avocado, salt, and curry powder mix gently.
3. Add tapioca starch and mix well again.
4. Make 8 salmon patties out of this mixture, about a half-inch thick.
5. Place them on a baking sheet lined with wax paper and freeze them for 20 minutes|
6. Place ¼ cup tapioca starch and coconut flakes on a flat plate.
7. Dip the patties in the whisked egg, then coat the frozen patties in the starch and flakes.
8. Place half of the patties in each of the crisper plate and spray them with cooking oil
9. Return the crisper plate to the Ninja Foodi Dual Zone Air Fryer.
10. Choose the Air Fry mode for Zone 1 and set the temperature to 390 degrees F and the time to 17 minutes|
11. Select the "MATCH" button to copy the settings for Zone 2.
12. Initiate cooking by pressing the START/STOP button.
13. Flip the patties once cooked halfway through, then resume cooking.
14. Sauté arugula with spinach in coconut oil in a pan for 30 seconds.
15. Serve the patties with sautéed greens mixture

Cod With Jalapeño

Servings: 4
Cooking Time: 14 Minutes
Ingredients:
- 4 cod fillets, boneless
- 1 jalapeño, minced
- 1 tablespoon avocado oil
- ½ teaspoon minced garlic

Directions:
1. In the shallow bowl, mix minced jalapeño, avocado oil, and minced garlic.
2. Put the cod fillets in the two air fryer drawers in one layer and top with minced jalapeño mixture.
3. Cook the fish at 185°C for 7 minutes per side.

Tuna With Herbs

Servings: 4
Cooking Time: 17 Minutes
Ingredients:
- 1 tablespoon butter, melted
- 1 medium-sized leek, thinly sliced
- 1 tablespoon chicken stock
- 1 tablespoon dry white wine
- 455 g tuna
- ½ teaspoon red pepper flakes, crushed
- Sea salt and ground black pepper, to taste
- ½ teaspoon dried rosemary
- ½ teaspoon dried basil
- ½ teaspoon dried thyme
- 2 small ripe tomatoes, puréed
- 120 g Parmesan cheese, grated

Directions:
1. Melt ½ tablespoon of butter in a sauté pan over medium-high heat. Now, cook the leek and garlic until tender and aromatic. Add the stock and wine to deglaze the pan.
2. Preheat the air fryer to 190°C.
3. Grease a casserole dish with the remaining ½ tablespoon of melted butter. Place the fish in the casserole dish. Add the seasonings. Top with the sautéed leek mixture. Add the tomato purée. Cook for 10 minutes in the preheated air fryer. Top with grated Parmesan cheese; cook an additional 7 minutes until the crumbs are golden. Bon appétit!

Scallops Gratiné With Parmesan

Servings: 2
Cooking Time: 9 Minutes
Ingredients:
- Scallops:
- 120 ml single cream
- 45 g grated Parmesan cheese
- 235 g thinly sliced spring onions
- 5 g chopped fresh parsley
- 3 cloves garlic, minced
- ½ teaspoon kosher or coarse sea salt
- ½ teaspoon black pepper
- 455 g sea scallops
- Topping:
- 30 g panko bread crumbs
- 20 g grated Parmesan cheese
- Vegetable oil spray
- For Serving:
- Lemon wedges
- Crusty French bread (optional)

Directions:
1. For the scallops: In a baking pan, combine the single cream, cheese, spring onions, parsley, garlic, salt, and pepper. Stir in the scallops. 2. For the topping: In a small bowl, combine the bread crumbs and cheese. Sprinkle evenly over the scallops. Spray the topping with vegetable oil spray. 3. Place the pan in the zone 1 air fryer drawer. Set the temperature to 164°C for 6 minutes. Set the temperature to 204°C for 3 minutes until the topping has browned. 4. To serve: Squeeze the lemon wedges over the gratin and serve with crusty French bread, if desired.

Chili Lime Tilapia

Servings: 4
Cooking Time: 10 Minutes

Ingredients:
- 340g tilapia fillets
- 2 teaspoons chili powder
- 1 teaspoon cumin
- 1 teaspoon garlic powder
- ½ teaspoon oregano
- ½ teaspoon sea salt
- ¼ teaspoon black pepper
- Lime zest from 1 lime
- Juice of ½ lime

Directions:
1. Mix chili powder and other spices with lime juice and zest in a bowl.
2. Rub this spice mixture over the tilapia fillets.
3. Place two fillets in each air basket.
4. Return the air fryer basket to the Ninja Foodi 2 Baskets Air Fryer.
5. Choose the "Air Fry" mode for Zone 1 at 400 degrees F and 10 minutes of cooking time.
6. Select the "MATCH COOK" option to copy the settings for Zone 2.
7. Initiate cooking by pressing the START/PAUSE BUTTON.
8. Flip the tilapia fillets once cooked halfway through.
9. Serve warm.

Nutrition:
- (Per serving) Calories 275 | Fat 1.4g |Sodium 582mg | Carbs 31.5g | Fiber 1.1g | Sugar 0.1g | Protein 29.8g

Pecan-crusted Catfish Nuggets With "fried" Okra

Servings:4
Cooking Time: 17 Minutes

Ingredients:
- FOR THE CATFISH NUGGETS
- 1 cup whole milk
- 1 pound fresh catfish nuggets (or cut-up fillets)
- 1 large egg
- 2 to 3 dashes Louisiana-style hot sauce (optional)
- ¼ cup finely chopped pecans
- ½ cup all-purpose flour
- Nonstick cooking spray
- Tartar sauce, for serving (optional)
- FOR THE OKRA
- ½ cup fine yellow cornmeal
- ¼ cup all-purpose flour
- ½ teaspoon garlic powder
- ½ teaspoon paprika
- 1 teaspoon kosher salt
- 1 large egg
- 8 ounces frozen cut okra, thawed

- Nonstick cooking spray

Directions:
1. To prep the catfish: Pour the milk into a large zip-top bag. Add the catfish and turn to coat. Set in the refrigerator to soak for at least 1 hour or up to overnight.
2. Remove the fish from the milk, shaking off any excess liquid.
3. In a shallow dish, whisk together the egg and hot sauce (if using). In a second shallow dish, combine the pecans and flour.
4. Dip each piece of fish into the egg mixture, then into the nut mixture to coat. Gently press the nut mixture to adhere to the fish. Spritz each nugget with cooking spray.
5. To prep the okra: Set up a breading station with two small shallow bowls. In the first bowl, stir together the cornmeal, flour, garlic powder, paprika, and salt. In the second bowl, whisk the egg.
6. Dip the okra first in the cornmeal mixture, then the egg, then back into the cornmeal. Spritz with cooking spray.
7. To cook the catfish and okra: Install a crisper plate in each of the two baskets. Place the fish in a single layer in the Zone 1 basket and insert the basket in the unit. Place the okra in the Zone 2 basket and insert the basket in the unit.
8. Select Zone 1, select AIR FRY, set the temperature to 390°F, and set the timer to 17 minutes.
9. Select Zone 2, select AIR FRY, set the temperature to 400°F, and set the timer to 12 minutes. Select SMART FINISH.
10. Press START/PAUSE to begin cooking.
11. When cooking is complete, the fish should be cooked through and the okra golden brown and crispy. Serve hot.

Nutrition:
- (Per serving) Calories: 414; Total fat: 24g; Saturated fat: 2.5g; Carbohydrates: 30g; Fiber: 3g; Protein: 23g; Sodium: 569mg

Oyster Po'boy

Servings: 4
Cooking Time: 5 Minutes
Ingredients:
- 105 g plain flour
- 40 g yellow cornmeal
- 1 tablespoon Cajun seasoning
- 1 teaspoon salt
- 2 large eggs, beaten
- 1 teaspoon hot sauce
- 455 g pre-shucked oysters
- 1 (12-inch) French baguette, quartered and sliced horizontally
- Tartar Sauce, as needed
- 150 g shredded lettuce, divided
- 2 tomatoes, cut into slices
- Cooking spray

Directions:
1. In a shallow bowl, whisk the flour, cornmeal, Cajun seasoning, and salt until blended. In a second shallow bowl, whisk together the eggs and hot sauce.
2. One at a time, dip the oysters in the cornmeal mixture, the eggs, and again in the cornmeal, coating thoroughly.
3. Preheat the zone 1 air fryer drawer to 204°C. Line the zone 1 air fryer drawer with baking paper.
4. Place the oysters on the baking paper and spritz with oil.
5. Air fry for 2 minutes. Shake the drawer, spritz the oysters with oil, and air fry for 3 minutes more until lightly browned and crispy.
6. Spread each sandwich half with Tartar Sauce. Assemble the po'boys by layering each sandwich with fried oysters, ½ cup shredded lettuce, and 2 tomato slices.
7. Serve immediately.

Miso Salmon And Oyster Po'boy

Servings: 6
Cooking Time: 12 Minutes

Ingredients:
- Miso Salmon:
- 2 tablespoons brown sugar
- 2 tablespoons soy sauce
- 2 tablespoons white miso paste
- 1 teaspoon minced garlic
- 1 teaspoon minced fresh ginger
- ½ teaspoon freshly cracked black pepper
- 2 salmon fillets, 140 g each
- Vegetable oil spray
- 1 teaspoon sesame seeds
- 2 spring onions, thinly sliced, for garnish
- Oyster Po'Boy:
- 105 g plain flour
- 40 g yellow cornmeal
- 1 tablespoon Cajun seasoning
- 1 teaspoon salt
- 2 large eggs, beaten
- 1 teaspoon hot sauce
- 455 g pre-shucked oysters
- 1 (12-inch) French baguette, quartered and sliced horizontally
- Tartar Sauce, as needed
- 150 g shredded lettuce, divided
- 2 tomatoes, cut into slices
- Cooking spray

Directions:
1. Make the Miso Salmon :
2. In a small bowl, whisk together the brown sugar, soy sauce, miso, garlic, ginger, and pepper to combine.
3. Place the salmon fillets on a plate. Pour half the sauce over the fillets; turn the fillets to coat the other sides with sauce.
4. Spray the zone 1 air fryer basket with vegetable oil spray. Place the sauce-covered salmon in the basket. Set the air fryer to 205°C for 12 minutes. Halfway through the cooking time, brush additional miso sauce on the salmon.
5. Sprinkle the salmon with the sesame seeds and spring onions and serve.
6. Make the Oyster Po'Boy :
7. In a shallow bowl, whisk the flour, cornmeal, Cajun seasoning, and salt until blended. In a second shallow bowl, whisk together the eggs and hot sauce.
8. One at a time, dip the oysters in the cornmeal mixture, the eggs, and again in the cornmeal, coating thoroughly.
9. Preheat the air fryer to 205°C. Line the zone 2 air fryer basket with baking paper.
10. Place the oysters on the baking paper and spritz with oil.
11. Air fry for 2 minutes. Shake the basket, spritz the oysters with oil, and air fry for 3 minutes more until lightly browned and crispy.
12. Spread each sandwich half with Tartar Sauce. Assemble the po'boys by layering each sandwich with fried oysters, ½ cup shredded lettuce, and 2 tomato slices.
13. Serve immediately.

Seasoned Tuna Steaks

Servings: 4
Cooking Time: 9 Minutes
Ingredients:
- 1 teaspoon garlic powder
- ½ teaspoon salt
- ¼ teaspoon dried thyme
- ¼ teaspoon dried oregano
- 4 tuna steaks
- 2 tablespoons olive oil
- 1 lemon, quartered

Directions:
1. Preheat the air fryer to 190°C.
2. In a small bowl, whisk together the garlic powder, salt, thyme, and oregano.
3. Coat the tuna steaks with olive oil. Season both sides of each steak with the seasoning blend. Place the steaks in a single layer in the two air fryer baskets.
4. Roast for 5 minutes, then flip and roast for an additional 3 to 4 minutes.

Poultry Recipes

Honey Butter Chicken

Servings: 4
Cooking Time: 15 Minutes
Ingredients:
- 4 chicken breasts, boneless
- 85g honey
- 28g butter, melted
- 2 tsp lemon juice
- 15ml olive oil
- 62g Dijon mustard
- Pepper
- Salt

Directions:
1. In a small bowl, mix butter, oil, lemon juice, honey, mustard, pepper, and salt.
2. Insert a crisper plate in the Ninja Foodi air fryer baskets.
3. Brush chicken breasts with butter mixture and place them in both baskets.
4. Select zone 1 then select "bake" mode and set the temperature to 380 degrees F for 15 minutes. Press "match" to match zone 2 settings to zone 1. Press "start/stop" to begin.

Nutrition:
- (Per serving) Calories 434 | Fat 20.7g | Sodium 384mg | Carbs 18.4g | Fiber 0.6g | Sugar 17.6g | Protein 43.1g

Pecan-crusted Chicken Tenders

Servings: 4
Cooking Time: 12 Minutes

Ingredients:
- 2 tablespoons mayonnaise
- 1 teaspoon Dijon mustard
- 455 g boneless, skinless chicken tenders
- ½ teaspoon salt
- ¼ teaspoon ground black pepper
- 75 g chopped roasted pecans, finely ground

Directions:
1. In a small bowl, whisk mayonnaise and mustard until combined. Brush mixture onto chicken tenders on both sides, then sprinkle tenders with salt and pepper.
2. Place pecans in a medium bowl and press each tender into pecans to coat each side.
3. Place tenders into the two ungreased air fryer drawers in a single layer. Adjust the temperature to 190°C and roast for 12 minutes, turning tenders halfway through cooking. Tenders will be golden brown and have an internal temperature of at least 76°C when done. Serve warm.

Crumbed Chicken Katsu

Servings: 4
Cooking Time: 26 Minutes

Ingredients:
- 1 lb. boneless chicken breast, cut in half
- 2 large eggs, beaten
- 1 ½ cups panko bread crumbs
- Salt and black pepper ground to taste
- Cooking spray
- Sauce:
- 1 tablespoon sugar
- 2 tablespoons soy sauce
- 1 tablespoon sherry
- ½ cup ketchup
- 2 teaspoons Worcestershire sauce
- 1 teaspoon garlic, minced

Directions:
1. Mix soy sauce, ketchup, sherry, sugar, garlic, and Worcestershire sauce in a mixing bowl.
2. Keep this katsu aside for a while.
3. Rub the chicken pieces with salt and black pepper.
4. Whisk eggs in a shallow dish and spread breadcrumbs in another tray.
5. Dip the chicken in the egg mixture and coat them with breadcrumbs.
6. Place the coated chicken in the two crisper plates and spray them with cooking spray.
7. Return the crisper plate to the Ninja Foodi Dual Zone Air Fryer.
8. Choose the Air Fry mode for Zone 1 and set the temperature to 390 degrees F and the time to 26 minutes
9. Select the "MATCH" button to copy the settings for Zone 2.
10. Initiate cooking by pressing the START/STOP button.
11. Flip the chicken once cooked halfway through, then resume cooking.
12. Serve warm with the sauce.

Asian Chicken Drumsticks

Servings: 4
Cooking Time: 20 Minutes
Ingredients:
- 8 chicken drumsticks
- 1 lime juice
- 30ml rice wine
- 45ml fish sauce
- 2 tbsp garlic, minced
- 55g brown sugar
- ½ tsp Sriracha sauce
- 1 tsp black pepper
- 1 tsp sesame oil
- Salt

Directions:
1. Add chicken drumsticks and remaining ingredients into the bowl and mix well. Cover and place in refrigerator for 4 hours.
2. Insert a crisper plate in the Ninja Foodi air fryer baskets.
3. Place the marinated chicken drumsticks in both baskets.
4. Select zone 1, then select "air fry" mode and set the temperature to 360 degrees F for 20 minutes. Press "match" to match zone 2 settings to zone 1. Press "start/stop" to begin.

Nutrition:
- (Per serving) Calories 225 | Fat 6.4g | Sodium 1223mg | Carbs 14.6g | Fiber 0.2g | Sugar 11.3g | Protein 26.3g

Stuffed Chicken Florentine

Servings: 4
Cooking Time: 20 Minutes
Ingredients:
- 3 tablespoons pine nuts
- 40 g frozen spinach, thawed and squeezed dry
- 75 g ricotta cheese
- 2 tablespoons grated Parmesan cheese
- 3 cloves garlic, minced
- Salt and freshly ground black pepper, to taste
- 4 small boneless, skinless chicken breast halves (about 680 g)
- 8 slices bacon

Directions:
1. In a large bowl, combine the spinach, ricotta, Parmesan, and garlic. Season to taste with salt and pepper and stir well until thoroughly combined.
2. Using a sharp knife, cut into the chicken breasts, slicing them across and opening them up like a book, but be careful not to cut them all the way through. Sprinkle the chicken with salt and pepper.
3. Spoon equal amounts of the spinach mixture into the chicken, then fold the top of the chicken breast back over the top of the stuffing. Wrap each chicken breast with 2 slices of bacon.
4. Air fry the chicken for 18 to 20 minutes in zone 1 drawer until the bacon is crisp and a thermometer inserted into the thickest part of the chicken registers 76°C.
5. Place the pine nuts in a small pan and set in the zone 2 air fryer drawer. Air fry at 200°C for 2 to 3 minutes until toasted. Remove the pine nuts to a mixing bowl.

Bbq Cheddar-stuffed Chicken Breasts

Servings: 2
Cooking Time: 25 Minutes
Ingredients:
- 3 strips cooked bacon, divided
- 2 ounces cheddar cheese, cubed, divided
- ¼ cup BBQ sauce, divided
- 2 (4-ounces) skinless, boneless chicken breasts
- Salt and ground black pepper, to taste

Directions:
1. In a mixing bowl, combine the cooked bacon, cheddar cheese, and 1 tablespoon BBQ sauce.
2. Make a horizontal 1-inch cut at the top of each chicken breast with a long, sharp knife, producing a little interior pouch. Fill each breast with an equal amount of the bacon-cheese mixture. Wrap the remaining bacon strips around each chicken breast. Coat the chicken breasts with the leftover BBQ sauce and lay them in a baking dish.
3. Install a crisper plate in both drawers. Place half the chicken breasts in zone 1 and half in zone 2, then insert the drawers into the unit.
4. Select zone 1, select AIR FRY, set temperature to 390 degrees F/ 200 degrees C, and set time to 22 minutes. Select MATCH to match zone 2 settings to zone 1. Press the START/STOP button to begin cooking.
5. When the time reaches 11 minutes, press START/STOP to pause the unit. Remove the drawers and flip the chicken. Re-insert drawers into the unit and press START/STOP to resume cooking.
6. When cooking is complete, remove the chicken breasts.

Nutrition:
- (Per serving) Calories 379 | Fat 12.8g | Sodium 906mg | Carbs 11.1g | Fiber 0.4g | Sugar 8.3g | Protein 37.7g

Cornish Hen With Baked Potatoes

Servings: 2
Cooking Time: 45
Ingredients:
- Salt, to taste
- 1 large potato
- 1 tablespoon of avocado oil
- 1.5 pounds of Cornish hen, skinless and whole
- 2-3 teaspoons of poultry seasoning, dry rub

Directions:
1. Take a fork and pierce the large potato.
2. Rub the potato with avocado oil and salt.
3. Now put the potatoes in the first basket.
4. Now pick the Cornish hen and season the hen with poultry seasoning (dry rub) and salt.
5. Remember to coat the whole Cornish hen well.
6. Put the potato in zone 1 basket.
7. Now place the hen into zone 2 baskets.
8. Now hit 1 for the first basket and set it to AIR FRY mode at 350 degrees F, for 45 minutes.
9. For the second basket hit 2 and set the time to 45 minutes at 350 degrees F.
10. To start cooking, hit the smart finish button and press hit start.
11. Once the cooking cycle complete, turn off the air fryer and take out the potatoes and Cornish hen from both air fryer baskets.
12. Serve hot and enjoy.

Nutrition:
- (Per serving) Calories 612 | Fat 14.3 g | Sodium 304mg | Carbs 33.4 g | Fiber 4.5 g | Sugar 1.5g | Protein 83.2 g

Harissa-rubbed Chicken

Servings: 4
Cooking Time: 21 Minutes
Ingredients:
- Harissa:
- 120 ml olive oil
- 6 cloves garlic, minced
- 2 tablespoons smoked paprika
- 1 tablespoon ground coriander
- 1 tablespoon ground cumin
- 1 teaspoon ground caraway
- 1 teaspoon kosher salt
- ½ to 1 teaspoon cayenne pepper
- Chickens:
- 120 g yogurt
- 2 small chickens, any giblets removed, split in half lengthwise

Directions:
1. For the harissa: In a medium microwave-safe bowl, combine the oil, garlic, paprika, coriander, cumin, caraway, salt, and cayenne. Microwave on high for 1 minute, stirring halfway through the cooking time. 2. For the chicken: In a small bowl, combine 1 to 2 tablespoons harissa and the yogurt. Whisk until well combined. Place the chicken halves in a resealable plastic bag and pour the marinade over. Seal the bag and massage until all of the pieces are thoroughly coated. Marinate at room temperature for 30 minutes or in the refrigerator for up to 24 hours. 3. Arrange the hen halves in a single layer in the two air fryer drawers. Set the air fryer to 200°C for 20 minutes. Use a meat thermometer to ensure the chickens have reached an internal temperature of 76°C.

Ranch Turkey Tenders With Roasted Vegetable Salad

Servings: 4
Cooking Time: 20 Minutes
Ingredients:
- FOR THE TURKEY TENDERS
- 1 pound turkey tenderloin
- ¼ cup ranch dressing
- ½ cup panko bread crumbs
- Nonstick cooking spray
- FOR THE VEGETABLE SALAD
- 1 large sweet potato, peeled and diced
- 1 zucchini, diced
- 1 red bell pepper, diced
- 1 small red onion, sliced
- 1 tablespoon vegetable oil
- ¼ teaspoon kosher salt
- ½ teaspoon freshly ground black pepper
- 2 cups baby spinach
- ½ cup store-bought balsamic vinaigrette
- ¼ cup chopped walnuts

Directions:

1. To prep the turkey tenders: Slice the turkey crosswise into 16 strips. Brush both sides of each strip with ranch dressing, then coat with the panko. Press the bread crumbs into the turkey to help them adhere. Mist both sides of the strips with cooking spray.
2. To prep the vegetables: In a large bowl, combine the sweet potato, zucchini, bell pepper, onion, and vegetable oil. Stir well to coat the vegetables. Season with the salt and black pepper.
3. To cook the turkey and vegetables:
4. Install a crisper plate in the Zone 1 basket. Place the turkey tenders in the basket in a single layer and insert the basket in the unit. Place the vegetables in the Zone 2 basket and insert the basket in the unit.
5. Select Zone 1, select AIR FRY, set the temperature to 375°F, and set the time to 20 minutes.
6. Select Zone 2, select ROAST, set the temperature to 400°F, and set the time to 20 minutes. Select SMART FINISH.
7. Press START/PAUSE to begin cooking.
8. When both timers read 10 minutes, press START/PAUSE. Remove the Zone 1 basket and use silicone-tipped tongs to flip the turkey tenders. Reinsert the basket in the unit. Remove the Zone 2 basket and shake to redistribute the vegetables. Reinsert the basket and press START/PAUSE to resume cooking.
9. When cooking is complete, the turkey will be golden brown and cooked through and the vegetables will be fork-tender.
10. Place the spinach in a large serving bowl. Mix in the roasted vegetables and balsamic vinaigrette. Sprinkle with walnuts. Serve warm with the turkey tenders.

Indian Fennel Chicken

Servings: 4
Cooking Time: 15 Minutes
Ingredients:
- 450 g boneless, skinless chicken thighs, cut crosswise into thirds
- 1 yellow onion, cut into 1½-inch-thick slices
- 1 tablespoon coconut oil, melted
- 2 teaspoons minced fresh ginger
- 2 teaspoons minced garlic
- 1 teaspoon smoked paprika
- 1 teaspoon ground fennel
- 1 teaspoon garam masala
- 1 teaspoon ground turmeric
- 1 teaspoon kosher salt
- ½ to 1 teaspoon cayenne pepper
- Vegetable oil spray
- 2 teaspoons fresh lemon juice
- 5 g chopped fresh coriander or parsley

Directions:
1. Use a fork to pierce the chicken all over to allow the marinade to penetrate better.
2. In a large bowl, combine the onion, coconut oil, ginger, garlic, paprika, fennel, garam masala, turmeric, salt, and cayenne. Add the chicken, toss to combine, and marinate at room temperature for 30 minutes, or cover and refrigerate for up to 24 hours.
3. Place the chicken and onion in the zone 1 air fryer drawer. Spray with some vegetable oil spray. Set the air fryer to 180°C for 15 minutes. Halfway through the cooking time, remove the drawer, spray the chicken and onion with more vegetable oil spray, and toss gently to coat. At the end of the cooking time, use a meat thermometer to ensure the chicken has reached an internal temperature of 76°C.
4. Transfer the chicken and onion to a serving platter. Sprinkle with the lemon juice and coriander and serve.

Tex-mex Chicken Roll-ups

Servings: 8
Cooking Time: 14 To 17 Minutes
Ingredients:
- 900 g boneless, skinless chicken breasts or thighs
- 1 teaspoon chili powder
- ½ teaspoon smoked paprika
- ½ teaspoon ground cumin
- Sea salt and freshly ground black pepper, to taste
- 170 g Monterey Jack cheese, shredded
- 115 g canned diced green chilies
- Avocado oil spray

Directions:
1. Place the chicken in a large zip-top bag or between two pieces of plastic wrap. Using a meat mallet or heavy skillet, pound the chicken until it is about ¼ inch thick.
2. In a small bowl, combine the chili powder, smoked paprika, cumin, and salt and pepper to taste. Sprinkle both sides of the chicken with the seasonings.
3. Sprinkle the chicken with the Monterey Jack cheese, then the diced green chilies.
4. Roll up each piece of chicken from the long side, tucking in the ends as you go. Secure the roll-up with a toothpick.
5. Set the air fryer to 180ºC. . Spray the outside of the chicken with avocado oil. Place the chicken in a single layer in the two baskets, and roast for 7 minutes. Flip and cook for another 7 to 10 minutes, until an instant-read thermometer reads 70ºC.
6. Remove the chicken from the air fryer and allow it to rest for about 5 minutes before serving.

Almond Chicken

Servings: 4
Cooking Time: 25 Minutes
Ingredients:
- 2 large eggs
- ½ cup buttermilk
- 2 teaspoons garlic salt
- 1 teaspoon pepper
- 2 cups slivered almonds, finely chopped
- 4 boneless, skinless chicken breast halves (6 ounces each)

Directions:
1. Whisk together the egg, buttermilk, garlic salt, and pepper in a small bowl.
2. In another small bowl, place the almonds.
3. Dip the chicken in the egg mixture, then roll it in the almonds, patting it down to help the coating stick.
4. Install a crisper plate in both drawers. Place half the chicken breasts in the zone 1 drawer and half in zone 2's, then insert the drawers into the unit.
5. Select zone 1, select AIR FRY, set temperature to 390 degrees F/ 200 degrees C, and set time to 22 minutes. Select MATCH to match zone 2 settings to zone 1. Press the START/STOP button to begin cooking.
6. When the time reaches 11 minutes, press START/STOP to pause the unit. Remove the drawers and flip the chicken. Re-insert the drawers into the unit and press START/STOP to resume cooking.
7. When cooking is complete, remove the chicken.

Nutrition:
- (Per serving) Calories 353 | Fat 18g | Sodium 230mg | Carbs 6g | Fiber 2g | Sugar 3g | Protein 41g

Crispy Ranch Nuggets

Servings: 4
Cooking Time: 10 Minutes

Ingredients:
- 1 pound chicken tenders, cut into 1½–2-inch pieces
- 1 (1-ounce) sachet dry ranch salad dressing mix
- 2 tablespoons flour
- 1 egg
- 1 cup panko breadcrumbs
- Olive oil cooking spray

Directions:
1. Toss the chicken with the ranch seasoning in a large mixing bowl. Allow for 5–10 minutes of resting time.
2. Fill a resalable bag halfway with the flour.
3. Crack the egg into a small bowl and lightly beat it.
4. Spread the breadcrumbs onto a dish.
5. Toss the chicken in the bag to coat it. Dip the chicken in the egg mixture lightly, allowing excess to drain off. Roll the chicken pieces in the breadcrumbs, pressing them in, so they stick. Lightly spray with the cooking spray.
6. Install a crisper plate in both drawers. Place half the chicken tenders in the zone 1 drawer and half in the zone 2 one, then insert the drawers into the unit.
7. Select zone 1, select AIR FRY, set temperature to 390 degrees F/ 200 degrees C, and set time to 10 minutes. Select MATCH to match zone 2 settings to zone 1. Press the START/STOP button to begin cooking.
8. When the time reaches 6 minutes, press START/STOP to pause the unit. Remove the drawers and flip the chicken. Re-insert the drawers into the unit and press START/STOP to resume cooking.
9. When cooking is complete, remove the chicken.

Nutrition:
- (Per serving) Calories 244 | Fat 3.6g | Sodium 713mg | Carbs 25.3g | Fiber 0.1g | Sugar 0.1g | Protein 31g

Greek Chicken Meatballs

Servings: 4
Cooking Time: 9 Minutes

Ingredients:
- 455g ground chicken
- 1 large egg
- 1½ tablespoons garlic paste
- 1 tablespoon dried oregano
- 1 teaspoon lemon zest
- 1 teaspoon dried onion powder
- ¾ teaspoon salt
- ¼ teaspoon black pepper
- Oil spray

Directions:
1. Mix ground chicken with rest of the ingredients in a bowl.
2. Make 1-inch sized meatballs out of this mixture.
3. Place the meatballs in the air fryer baskets.
4. Return the air fryer basket 1 to Zone 1, and basket 2 to Zone 2 of the Ninja Foodi 2-Basket Air Fryer.
5. Choose the "Air Fry" mode for Zone 1 and set the temperature to 390 degrees F and 9 minutes of cooking time.
6. Select the "MATCH COOK" option to copy the settings for Zone 2.
7. Initiate cooking by pressing the START/PAUSE BUTTON.
8. Serve warm.

Nutrition:
- (Per serving) Calories 346 | Fat 16.1g | Sodium 882mg | Carbs 1.3g | Fiber 0.5g | Sugar 0.5g | Protein 48.2g

Buffalo Chicken

Servings: 4
Cooking Time: 22 Minutes
Ingredients:
- ½ cup plain fat-free Greek yogurt
- ¼ cup egg substitute
- 1 tablespoon plus 1 teaspoon hot sauce
- 1 cup panko breadcrumbs
- 1 tablespoon sweet paprika
- 1 tablespoon garlic pepper seasoning
- 1 tablespoon cayenne pepper
- 1-pound skinless, boneless chicken breasts, cut into 1-inch strips

Directions:
1. Combine the Greek yogurt, egg substitute, and hot sauce in a mixing bowl.
2. In a separate bowl, combine the panko breadcrumbs, paprika, garlic powder, and cayenne pepper.
3. Dip the chicken strips in the yogurt mixture, then coat them in the breadcrumb mixture.
4. Install a crisper plate in both drawers. Place the chicken strips into the drawers and then insert the drawers into the unit.
5. Select zone 1, select AIR FRY, set temperature to 390 degrees F/ 200 degrees C, and set time to 22 minutes. Select MATCH to match zone 2 settings to zone 1. Press the START/STOP button to begin cooking.
6. When cooking is complete, serve immediately.

Nutrition:
- (Per serving) Calories 234 | Fat 15.8g | Sodium 696mg | Carbs 22.1g | Fiber 1.1g | Sugar 1.7g | Protein 31.2g

Crusted Chicken Breast

Servings: 4
Cooking Time: 28 Minutes
Ingredients:
- 2 large eggs, beaten
- ½ cup all-purpose flour
- 1 ¼ cups panko bread crumbs
- ⅔ cup Parmesan, grated
- 4 teaspoons lemon zest
- 2 teaspoons dried oregano
- Salt, to taste
- 1 teaspoon cayenne pepper
- Freshly black pepper, to taste
- 4 boneless skinless chicken breasts

Directions:
1. Beat eggs in one shallow bowl and spread flour in another shallow bowl.
2. Mix panko with oregano, lemon zest, Parmesan, cayenne, oregano, salt, and black pepper in another shallow bowl.
3. First, coat the chicken with flour first, then dip it in the eggs and coat them with panko mixture.
4. Arrange the prepared chicken in the two crisper plates.
5. Return the crisper plate to the Ninja Foodi Dual Zone Air Fryer.
6. Choose the Air Fry mode for Zone 1 and set the temperature to 390 degrees F and the time to 28 minutes|
7. Select the "MATCH" button to copy the settings for Zone 2.
8. Initiate cooking by pressing the START/STOP button.
9. Flip the half-cooked chicken and continue cooking for 5 minutes until golden.
10. Serve warm.

Chipotle Drumsticks

Servings: 4
Cooking Time: 20 Minutes

Ingredients:
- 1 tablespoon tomato paste
- ½ teaspoon chipotle powder
- ¼ teaspoon apple cider vinegar
- ¼ teaspoon garlic powder
- 8 chicken drumsticks
- ½ teaspoon salt
- ⅛ teaspoon ground black pepper

Directions:
1. In a small bowl, combine tomato paste, chipotle powder, vinegar, and garlic powder.
2. Sprinkle drumsticks with salt and pepper, then place into a large bowl and pour in tomato paste mixture. Toss or stir to evenly coat all drumsticks in mixture.
3. Place drumsticks into two ungreased air fryer baskets. Adjust the temperature to 200°C and air fry for 25 minutes, turning drumsticks halfway through cooking. Drumsticks will be dark red with an internal temperature of at least 75°C when done. Serve warm.

Thai Chicken Meatballs

Servings: 4
Cooking Time: 10 Minutes

Ingredients:
- ½ cup sweet chili sauce
- 2 tablespoons lime juice
- 2 tablespoons ketchup
- 1 teaspoon soy sauce
- 1 large egg, lightly beaten
- ¾ cup panko breadcrumbs
- 1 green onion, finely chopped
- 1 tablespoon minced fresh cilantro
- ½ teaspoon salt
- ½ teaspoon garlic powder
- 1-pound lean ground chicken

Directions:
1. Combine the chili sauce, lime juice, ketchup, and soy sauce in a small bowl; set aside ½ cup for serving.
2. Combine the egg, breadcrumbs, green onion, cilantro, salt, garlic powder, and the remaining 4 tablespoons chili sauce mixture in a large mixing bowl. Mix in the chicken lightly yet thoroughly. Form into 12 balls.
3. Install a crisper plate in both drawers. Place half the chicken meatballs in the zone 1 drawer and half in zone 2's, then insert the drawers into the unit.
4. Select zone 1, select AIR FRY, set temperature to 390 degrees F/ 200 degrees C, and set time to 10 minutes. Select MATCH to match zone 2 settings to zone 1. Press the START/STOP button to begin cooking.
5. When the time reaches 5 minutes, press START/STOP to pause the unit. Remove the drawers and flip the chicken. Re-insert the drawers into the unit and press START/STOP to resume cooking.
6. When cooking is complete, remove the chicken meatballs and serve hot.

Nutrition:
- (Per serving) Calories 93 | Fat 3g | Sodium 369mg | Carbs 9g | Fiber 0g | Sugar 6g | Protein 9g

Greek Chicken Souvlaki

Servings: 3 To 4
Cooking Time: 15 Minutes
Ingredients:
- Chicken:
- Grated zest and juice of 1 lemon
- 2 tablespoons extra-virgin olive oil
- 1 tablespoon Greek souvlaki seasoning
- 450 g boneless, skinless chicken breast, cut into 2-inch chunks
- Vegetable oil spray
- For Serving:
- Warm pita bread or hot cooked rice
- Sliced ripe tomatoes
- Sliced cucumbers
- Thinly sliced red onion
- Kalamata olives
- Tzatziki

Directions:
1. For the chicken: In a small bowl, combine the lemon zest, lemon juice, olive oil, and souvlaki seasoning. Place the chicken in a gallon-size resealable plastic bag. Pour the marinade over chicken. Seal bag and massage to coat. Place the bag in a large bowl and marinate for 30 minutes, or cover and refrigerate up to 24 hours, turning the bag occasionally. 2. Place the chicken a single layer in the zone 1 air fryer drawer. Cook at 180ºC for 10 minutes, turning the chicken and spraying with a little vegetable oil spray halfway through the cooking time. Increase the air fryer temperature to 200ºC for 5 minutes to allow the chicken to crisp and brown a little. 3. Transfer the chicken to a serving platter and serve with pita bread or rice, tomatoes, cucumbers, onion, olives and tzatziki.

Chicken Bites

Servings: 4
Cooking Time: 20 Minutes
Ingredients:
- 900g chicken thighs, cut into chunks
- ¼ tsp white pepper
- ½ tsp onion powder
- 30ml olive oil
- 59ml fresh lemon juice
- ½ tsp garlic powder
- Pepper
- Salt

Directions:
1. Add chicken chunks and remaining ingredients into the bowl and mix well.
2. Cover the bowl and place it in the refrigerator overnight.
3. Insert a crisper plate in the Ninja Foodi air fryer baskets.
4. Place the marinated chicken in both baskets.
5. Select zone 1 then select "air fry" mode and set the temperature to 380 degrees F for 20 minutes. Press "match" to match zone 2 settings to zone 1. Press "start/stop" to begin.

Nutrition:
- (Per serving) Calories 497 | Fat 23.9g |Sodium 237mg | Carbs 0.9g | Fiber 0.2g | Sugar 0.5g | Protein 65.8g

Hawaiian Chicken Bites

Servings: 4
Cooking Time: 15 Minutes

Ingredients:
- 120 ml pineapple juice
- 2 tablespoons apple cider vinegar
- ½ tablespoon minced ginger
- 120 g ketchup
- 2 garlic cloves, minced
- 110 g brown sugar
- 2 tablespoons sherry
- 120 ml soy sauce
- 4 chicken breasts, cubed
- Cooking spray

Directions:
1. Combine the pineapple juice, cider vinegar, ginger, ketchup, garlic, and sugar in a saucepan. Stir to mix well. Heat over low heat for 5 minutes or until thickened. Fold in the sherry and soy sauce.
2. Dunk the chicken cubes in the mixture. Press to submerge. Wrap the bowl in plastic and refrigerate to marinate for at least an hour.
3. Preheat the air fryer to 180°C. Spritz the two air fryer drawers with cooking spray.
4. Remove the chicken cubes from the marinade. Shake the excess off and put in the preheated air fryer. Spritz with cooking spray.
5. Air fry for 15 minutes or until the chicken cubes are glazed and well browned. Shake the drawer at least three times during the frying.
6. Serve immediately.

Chicken & Broccoli

Servings: 4
Cooking Time: 20 Minutes

Ingredients:
- 450g chicken breasts, boneless & cut into 1-inch pieces
- 1 tsp sesame oil
- 15ml soy sauce
- 1 tsp garlic powder
- 45ml olive oil
- 350g broccoli florets
- 2 tsp hot sauce
- 2 tsp rice vinegar
- Pepper
- Salt

Directions:
1. In a bowl, add chicken, broccoli florets, and remaining ingredients and mix well.
2. Insert a crisper plate in the Ninja Foodi air fryer baskets.
3. Add the chicken and broccoli mixture in both baskets.
4. Select zone 1, then select "air fry" mode and set the temperature to 380 degrees F for 20 minutes. Press "match" and press "start/stop" to begin.

Nutrition:
- (Per serving) Calories 337 | Fat 20.2g | Sodium 440mg | Carbs 3.9g | Fiber 1.3g | Sugar 1g | Protein 34.5g

Chicken Thighs In Waffles

Servings: 4
Cooking Time: 40 Minutes
Ingredients:
- For the chicken:
- 4 chicken thighs, skin on
- 240 ml low-fat buttermilk
- 65 g all-purpose flour
- ½ teaspoon garlic powder
- ½ teaspoon mustard powder
- 1 teaspoon kosher salt
- ½ teaspoon freshly ground black pepper
- 85 g honey, for serving
- Cooking spray
- For the waffles:
- 65 g all-purpose flour
- 65 g whole wheat pastry flour
- 1 large egg, beaten
- 240 ml low-fat buttermilk
- 1 teaspoon baking powder
- 2 tablespoons rapeseed oil
- ½ teaspoon kosher salt
- 1 tablespoon granulated sugar

Directions:
1. Combine the chicken thighs with buttermilk in a large bowl. Wrap the bowl in plastic and refrigerate to marinate for at least an hour. 2. Preheat the air fryer to 180°C. Spritz the two air fryer baskets with cooking spray. 3. Combine the flour, mustard powder, garlic powder, salt, and black pepper in a shallow dish. Stir to mix well. 4. Remove the thighs from the buttermilk and pat dry with paper towels. Sit the bowl of buttermilk aside. 5. Dip the thighs in the flour mixture first, then into the buttermilk, and then into the flour mixture. Shake the excess off. 6. Arrange the thighs in the two preheated air fryer baskets and spritz with cooking spray. Air fryer for 20 minutes or until an instant-read thermometer inserted in the thickest part of the chicken thighs registers at least 75°C. Flip the thighs halfway through. 7. Meanwhile, make the waffles: combine the ingredients for the waffles in a large bowl. Stir to mix well, then arrange the mixture in a waffle iron and cook until a golden and fragrant waffle forms. 8. Remove the waffles from the waffle iron and slice into 4 pieces. Remove the chicken thighs from the air fryer and allow to cool for 5 minutes. 9. Arrange each chicken thigh on each waffle piece and drizzle with 1 tablespoon of honey. Serve warm.

Easy Cajun Chicken Drumsticks

Servings: 5
Cooking Time: 40 Minutes
Ingredients:
- 1 tablespoon olive oil
- 10 chicken drumsticks
- 1½ tablespoons Cajun seasoning
- Salt and ground black pepper, to taste

Directions:
1. Preheat the air fryer to 200°C. Grease the two air fryer drawers with olive oil. 2. On a clean work surface, rub the chicken drumsticks with Cajun seasoning, salt, and ground black pepper. 3. Arrange the seasoned chicken drumsticks in a single layer in the air fryer. 4. Air fry for 18 minutes or until lightly browned. Flip the drumsticks halfway through. 5. Remove the chicken drumsticks from the air fryer. Serve immediately.

Cornish Hen With Asparagus

Servings: 2
Cooking Time: 45
Ingredients:
- 10 spears of asparagus
- Salt and black pepper, to taste
- 1 Cornish hen
- Salt, to taste
- Black pepper, to taste
- 1 teaspoon of Paprika
- Coconut spray, for greasing
- 2 lemons, sliced

Directions:
1. Wash and pat dry the asparagus and coat it with coconut oil spray.
2. Sprinkle salt on the asparagus and place inside the first basket of the air fryer.
3. Next, take the Cornish hen and rub it well with the salt, black pepper, and paprika.
4. Oil sprays the Cornish hen and place in the second air fryer basket.
5. Press button 1 for the first basket and set it to AIR FRY mode at 350 degrees F, for 8 minutes.
6. For the second basket hit 2 and set the time to 45 minutes at 350 degrees F, by selecting the ROAST mode.
7. To start cooking, hit the smart finish button and press hit start.
8. Once the 6 minutes pass press 1 and pause and take out the asparagus.
9. Once the chicken cooking cycle complete, press 2 and hit pause.
10. Take out the Basket of chicken and let it transfer to the serving plate
11. Serve the chicken with roasted asparagus and slices of lemon.
12. Serve hot and enjoy.

Nutrition:
- (Per serving) Calories 192| Fat 4.7g| Sodium 151mg | Carbs10.7 g | Fiber 4.6g | Sugar 3.8g | Protein 30g

Yummy Chicken Breasts

Servings: 2
Cooking Time: 25
Ingredients:
- 4 large chicken breasts, 6 ounces each
- 2 tablespoons of oil bay seasoning
- 1 tablespoon Montreal chicken seasoning
- 1 teaspoon of thyme
- 1/2 teaspoon of paprika
- Salt, to taste
- oil spray, for greasing

Directions:
1. Season the chicken breast pieces with the listed seasoning and let them rest for 40 minutes.
2. Grease both sides of the chicken breast pieces with oil spray.
3. Divide the chicken breast piece between both baskets.
4. Set zone 1 to AIRFRY mode at 400 degrees F, for 15 minutes.
5. Select the MATCH button for another basket.
6. Select pause and take out the baskets and flip the chicken breast pieces, after 15 minutes.
7. Select the zones to 400 degrees F for 10 more minutes using the MATCH cook button.
8. Once it's done serve.

Nutrition:
- (Per serving) Calories 711| Fat 27.7g| Sodium 895mg | Carbs 1.6g | Fiber 0.4g | Sugar 0.1g | Protein 106.3g

Turkey Meatloaf With Veggie Medley

Servings: 4
Cooking Time: 30 Minutes

Ingredients:
- FOR THE MEATLOAF
- 1 large egg
- ¼ cup ketchup
- 2 teaspoons Worcestershire sauce
- ½ cup Italian-style bread crumbs
- 1 teaspoon kosher salt
- 1 pound ground turkey (93 percent lean)
- 1 tablespoon vegetable oil
- FOR THE VEGGIE MEDLEY
- 2 carrots, thinly sliced
- 8 ounces green beans, trimmed (about 2 cups)
- 2 cups broccoli florets
- 1 red bell pepper, sliced into strips
- 2 tablespoons vegetable oil
- ½ teaspoon kosher salt
- ½ teaspoon freshly ground black pepper

Directions:
1. To prep the meatloaf:
2. In a large bowl, whisk the egg. Stir in the ketchup, Worcestershire sauce, bread crumbs, and salt. Let sit for 5 minutes to allow the bread crumbs to absorb some moisture.
3. Gently mix in the turkey until just incorporated. Form the mixture into a loaf. Brush with the oil.
4. To prep the veggie medley: In a large bowl, combine the carrots, green beans, broccoli, bell pepper, oil, salt, and black pepper. Mix well to coat the vegetables with the oil.
5. To cook the meatloaf and veggie medley:
6. Install a crisper plate in each of the two baskets. Place the meatloaf in the Zone 1 basket and insert the basket in the unit. Place the vegetables in the Zone 2 basket and insert the basket in the unit.
7. Select Zone 1, select ROAST, set the temperature to 350°F, and set the time to 30 minutes.
8. Select Zone 2, select AIR FRY, set the temperature to 390°F, and set the time to 20 minutes. Select SMART FINISH.
9. Press START/PAUSE to begin cooking.
10. When cooking is complete, the meatloaf will be cooked through and the vegetables will be tender and roasted.

Beef, Pork, And Lamb Recipes

Stuffed Beef Fillet With Feta Cheese

Servings: 4
Cooking Time: 10 Minutes
Ingredients:
- 680 g beef fillet, pounded to ¼ inch thick
- 3 teaspoons sea salt
- 1 teaspoon ground black pepper
- 60 g creamy goat cheese
- 120 ml crumbled feta cheese
- 60 ml finely chopped onions
- 2 cloves garlic, minced
- Cooking spray

Directions:
1. Preheat the air fryer to 204°C. Spritz the two air fryer drawers with cooking spray. 2. Unfold the beef on a clean work surface. Rub the salt and pepper all over the beef to season. 3. Make the filling for the stuffed beef fillet: Combine the goat cheese, feta, onions, and garlic in a medium bowl. Stir until well blended. 4. Spoon the mixture in the center of the fillet. Roll the fillet up tightly like rolling a burrito and use some kitchen twine to tie the fillet. 5. Arrange the fillet in the two air fryer drawers and air fry for 10 minutes, flipping the fillet halfway through to ensure even cooking, or until an instant-read thermometer inserted in the center of the fillet registers 57°C for medium-rare. 6. Transfer to a platter and serve immediately.

Mojito Lamb Chops

Servings: 2
Cooking Time: 5 Minutes
Ingredients:
- Marinade:
- 2 teaspoons grated lime zest
- 120 ml lime juice
- 60 ml avocado oil
- 60 ml chopped fresh mint leaves
- 4 cloves garlic, roughly chopped
- 2 teaspoons fine sea salt
- ½ teaspoon ground black pepper
- 4 (1-inch-thick) lamb chops
- Sprigs of fresh mint, for garnish (optional)
- Lime slices, for serving (optional)

Directions:
1. Make the marinade: Place all the ingredients for the marinade in a food processor or blender and purée until mostly smooth with a few small chunks. Transfer half of the marinade to a shallow dish and set the other half aside for serving. Add the lamb to the shallow dish, cover, and place in the refrigerator to marinate for at least 2 hours or overnight. 2. Spray the two air fryer drawers with avocado oil. Preheat the air fryer to 200°C. 3. Remove the chops from the marinade and place them in the two air fryer drawers. Air fry for 5 minutes, or until the internal temperature reaches 64°C for medium doneness. 4. Allow the chops to rest for 10 minutes before serving with the rest of the marinade as a sauce. Garnish with fresh mint leaves and serve with lime slices, if desired. Best served fresh.

Spice-rubbed Pork Loin

Servings: 6
Cooking Time: 20 Minutes
Ingredients:
- 1 teaspoon paprika
- ½ teaspoon ground cumin
- ½ teaspoon chili powder
- ½ teaspoon garlic powder
- 2 tablespoons coconut oil
- 1 (680 g) boneless pork loin
- ½ teaspoon salt
- ¼ teaspoon ground black pepper

Directions:
1. In a small bowl, mix paprika, cumin, chili powder, and garlic powder.
2. Drizzle coconut oil over pork. Sprinkle pork loin with salt and pepper, then rub spice mixture evenly on all sides.
3. Place pork loin into the two ungreased air fryer drawer. Adjust the temperature to 204°C and air fry for 20 minutes, turning pork halfway through cooking. Pork loin will be browned and have an internal temperature of at least 64°C when done. Serve warm.

Steak And Asparagus Bundles

Servings: 6
Cooking Time: 10 Minutes
Ingredients:
- 907g flank steak, cut into 6 pieces
- Salt and black pepper, to taste
- ½ cup tamari sauce
- 2 cloves garlic, crushed
- 455g asparagus, trimmed
- 3 capsicums, sliced
- ¼ cup balsamic vinegar
- 79 ml beef broth
- 2 tablespoons unsalted butter
- Olive oil spray

Directions:
1. Mix steaks with black pepper, tamari sauce, and garlic in a Ziplock bag.
2. Seal the bag, shake well and refrigerate for 1 hour.
3. Place the steaks on the working surface and top each with asparagus and capsicums.
4. Roll the steaks and secure them with toothpicks.
5. Place these rolls in the air fryer baskets.
6. Return the air fryer basket 1 to Zone 1, and basket 2 to Zone 2 of the Ninja Foodi 2-Basket Air Fryer.
7. Choose the "Air Fry" mode for Zone 1 and set the temperature to 400 degrees F and 10 minutes of cooking time.
8. Select the "MATCH COOK" option to copy the settings for Zone 2.
9. Initiate cooking by pressing the START/PAUSE BUTTON.
10. Meanwhile, cook broth with butter and vinegar in a saucepan.
11. Cook this mixture until reduced by half and adjust seasoning with black pepper and salt.
12. Serve the steak rolls with the prepared sauce.

Rosemary Ribeye Steaks And Mongolian-style Beef

Servings: 6
Cooking Time: 15 Minutes

Ingredients:

- Rosemary Ribeye Steaks:
- 60 ml butter
- 1 clove garlic, minced
- Salt and ground black pepper, to taste
- 1½ tablespoons balsamic vinegar
- 60 ml rosemary, chopped
- 2 ribeye steaks
- Mongolian-Style Beef:
- Oil, for spraying
- 60 ml cornflour
- 450 g bavette or skirt steak, thinly sliced
- 180 ml packed light brown sugar
- 120 ml soy sauce
- 2 teaspoons toasted sesame oil
- 1 tablespoon minced garlic
- ½ teaspoon ground ginger
- 120 ml water
- Cooked white rice or ramen noodles, for serving

Directions:

1. Make the Rosemary Ribeye Steaks :
2. Melt the butter in a skillet over medium heat. Add the garlic and fry until fragrant.
3. Remove the skillet from the heat and add the salt, pepper, and vinegar. Allow it to cool.
4. Add the rosemary, then pour the mixture into a Ziploc bag.
5. Put the ribeye steaks in the bag and shake well, coating the meat well. Refrigerate for an hour, then allow to sit for a further twenty minutes.
6. Preheat the zone 1 air fryer drawer to 204°C.
7. Air fry the ribeye steaks for 15 minutes.
8. Take care when removing the steaks from the air fryer and plate up.
9. Serve immediately.
10. Make the Mongolian-Style Beef :
11. Line the zone 2 air fryer drawer with parchment and spray lightly with oil.
12. Place the cornflour in a bowl and dredge the steak until evenly coated. Shake off any excess cornflour.
13. Place the steak in the prepared drawer and spray lightly with oil.
14. Roast at 200°C for 5 minutes, flip, and cook for another 5 minutes.
15. In a small saucepan, combine the brown sugar, soy sauce, sesame oil, garlic, ginger, and water and bring to a boil over medium-high heat, stirring frequently. Remove from the heat.
16. Transfer the meat to the sauce and toss until evenly coated. Let sit for about 5 minutes so the steak absorbs the flavors. Serve with white rice or ramen noodles.

Chorizo And Beef Burger

Servings: 4
Cooking Time: 15 Minutes
Ingredients:
- 340 g 80/20 beef mince
- 110 g Mexican-style chorizo crumb
- 60 ml chopped onion
- 5 slices pickled jalapeños, chopped
- 2 teaspoons chili powder
- 1 teaspoon minced garlic
- ¼ teaspoon cumin

Directions:
1. In a large bowl, mix all ingredients. Divide the mixture into four sections and form them into burger patties.
2. Place burger patties into the two air fryer drawers.
3. Adjust the temperature to 192°C and air fry for 15 minutes.
4. Flip the patties halfway through the cooking time. Serve warm.

Lamb Chops With Dijon Garlic

Servings: 4
Cooking Time: 22 Minutes
Ingredients:
- 2 teaspoons Dijon mustard
- 2 teaspoons olive oil
- 1 teaspoon soy sauce
- 1 teaspoon garlic, minced
- 1 teaspoon cumin powder
- 1 teaspoon cayenne pepper
- 1 teaspoon Italian spice blend (optional)
- ¼ teaspoon salt
- 8 lamb chops

Directions:
1. Combine the Dijon mustard, olive oil, soy sauce, garlic, cumin powder, cayenne pepper, Italian spice blend (optional), and salt in a medium mixing bowl.
2. Put the marinade in a large Ziploc bag. Add the lamb chops. Seal the bag tightly after pressing out the air. Coat the lamb in the marinade by shaking the bag and pressing the chops into the mixture. Place in the fridge for at least 30 minutes, or up to overnight, to marinate.
3. Install a crisper plate in both drawers. Place half the lamb chops in the zone 1 drawer and half in zone 2's, then insert the drawers into the unit.
4. Select zone 1, select AIR FRY, set temperature to 390 degrees F/ 200 degrees C, and set time to 22 minutes. Select MATCH to match zone 2 settings to zone 1. Press the START/STOP button to begin cooking.
5. When the time reaches 11 minutes, press START/STOP to pause the unit. Remove the drawers and flip the lamb chops. Re-insert the drawers into the unit and press START/STOP to resume cooking.
6. Serve and enjoy!

Nutrition:
- (Per serving) Calories 343 | Fat 15.1g | Sodium 380mg | Carbs 0.9 g | Fiber 0.3g | Sugar 0.1g | Protein 48.9g

Tasty Lamb Patties

Servings: 8
Cooking Time: 12 Minutes
Ingredients:
- 900g ground lamb
- 1 tbsp ground coriander
- 4g fresh parsley, chopped
- 1 tsp garlic, minced
- ½ tsp cinnamon
- 1 tsp paprika
- 1 tbsp ground cumin
- Pepper
- Salt

Directions:
1. Add ground meat and remaining ingredients into a bowl and mix until well combined.
2. Insert a crisper plate in the Ninja Foodi air fryer baskets.
3. Make patties from the meat mixture and place in both baskets.
4. Select zone 1, then select "air fry" mode and set the temperature to 390 degrees F for 12 minutes. Press "match" to match zone 2 settings to zone 1. Press "start/stop" to begin. Turn halfway through.

Tomahawk Steak

Servings: 4
Cooking Time: 12 Minutes
Ingredients:
- 4 tablespoons butter, softened
- 2 cloves garlic, minced
- 2 teaspoons chopped fresh parsley
- 1 teaspoon chopped chives
- 1 teaspoon chopped fresh thyme
- 1 teaspoon chopped fresh rosemary
- 2 (2 pounds each) bone-in ribeye steaks
- Kosher salt, to taste
- Freshly ground black pepper, to taste

Directions:
1. In a small bowl, combine the butter and herbs. Place the mixture in the center of a piece of plastic wrap and roll it into a log. Twist the ends together to keep it tight and refrigerate until hardened, about 20 minutes.
2. Season the steaks on both sides with salt and pepper.
3. Install a crisper plate in both drawers. Place one steak in the zone 1 drawer and one in zone 2's, then insert the drawers into the unit.
4. Select zone 1, select AIR FRY, set temperature to 390 degrees F/ 200 degrees C, and set time to 12 minutes. Select MATCH to match zone 2 settings to zone 1. Press the START/STOP button to begin cooking.
5. When the time reaches 10 minutes, press START/STOP to pause the unit. Remove the drawers and flip the steaks. Add the herb-butter to the tops of the steaks. Re-insert the drawers into the unit and press START/STOP to resume cooking.
6. Serve and enjoy!

Nutrition:
- (Per serving) Calories 338 | Fat 21.2g | Sodium 1503mg | Carbs 5.1g | Fiber 0.3g | Sugar 4.6g | Protein 29.3g

Pork Chops With Brussels Sprouts

Servings: 4
Cooking Time: 15 Minutes.

Ingredients:

- 4 bone-in center-cut pork chop
- Cooking spray
- Salt, to taste
- Black pepper, to taste
- 2 teaspoons olive oil
- 2 teaspoons pure maple syrup
- 2 teaspoons Dijon mustard
- 6 ounces Brussels sprouts, quartered

Directions:

1. Rub pork chop with salt, ¼ teaspoons black pepper, and cooking spray.
2. Toss Brussels sprouts with mustard, syrup, oil, ¼ teaspoon of black pepper in a medium bowl.
3. Add pork chop to the crisper plate of Zone 1 of the Ninja Foodi Dual Zone Air Fryer.
4. Return the crisper plate to the Ninja Foodi Dual Zone Air Fryer.
5. Choose the Air Fry mode for Zone 1 and set the temperature to 400 degrees F and the time to 15 minutes.
6. Add the Brussels sprouts to the crisper plate of Zone 2 and return it to the unit.
7. Choose the Air Fry mode for Zone 2 with 350 degrees F and the time to 13 minutes.
8. Press the SYNC button to sync the finish time for both Zones.
9. Initiate cooking by pressing the START/STOP button.
10. Serve warm and fresh

Nutrition:

- (Per serving) Calories 336 | Fat 27.1g | Sodium 66mg | Carbs 1.1g | Fiber 0.4g | Sugar 0.2g | Protein 19.7g

Cheesesteak Taquitos

Servings: 8
Cooking Time: 12 Minutes

Ingredients:

- 1 pack soft corn tortillas
- 136g beef steak strips
- 2 green peppers, sliced
- 1 white onion, chopped
- 1 pkg dry Italian dressing mix
- 10 slices Provolone cheese
- Cooking spray or olive oil

Directions:

1. Mix beef with cooking oil, peppers, onion, and dressing mix in a bowl.
2. Divide the strips in the air fryer baskets.
3. Return the air fryer basket 1 to Zone 1, and basket 2 to Zone 2 of the Ninja Foodi 2-Basket Air Fryer.
4. Choose the "Air Fry" mode for Zone 1 at 375 degrees F and 12 minutes of cooking time.
5. Select the "MATCH COOK" option to copy the settings for Zone 2.
6. Initiate cooking by pressing the START/PAUSE BUTTON.
7. Flip the strips once cooked halfway through.
8. Divide the beef strips in the tortillas and top the beef with a beef slice.
9. Roll the tortillas and serve.

Steaks With Walnut-blue Cheese Butter

Servings: 6
Cooking Time: 10 Minutes
Ingredients:
- 120 ml unsalted butter, at room temperature
- 120 ml crumbled blue cheese
- 2 tablespoons finely chopped walnuts
- 1 tablespoon minced fresh rosemary
- 1 teaspoon minced garlic
- ¼ teaspoon cayenne pepper
- Sea salt and freshly ground black pepper, to taste
- 680 g sirloin steaks, at room temperature

Directions:
1. In a medium bowl, combine the butter, blue cheese, walnuts, rosemary, garlic, and cayenne pepper and salt and black pepper to taste. Use clean hands to ensure that everything is well combined. Place the mixture on a sheet of parchment paper and form it into a log. Wrap it tightly in plastic wrap. Refrigerate for at least 2 hours or freeze for 30 minutes.
2. Season the steaks generously with salt and pepper.
3. Set the air fryer to 204°C and let it preheat for 5 minutes.
4. Place the steaks in the two drawers in a single layer and air fry for 5 minutes. Flip the steaks, and cook for 5 minutes more, until an instant-read thermometer reads 49°C for medium-rare.
5. Transfer the steaks to a plate. Cut the butter into pieces and place the desired amount on top of the steaks. Tent a piece of aluminum foil over the steaks and allow to sit for 10 minutes before serving.
6. Store any remaining butter in a sealed container in the refrigerator for up to 2 weeks.

Mozzarella Stuffed Beef And Pork Meatballs

Servings: 4 To 6
Cooking Time: 12 Minutes
Ingredients:
- 1 tablespoon olive oil
- 1 small onion, finely chopped
- 1 to 2 cloves garlic, minced
- 340 g beef mince
- 340 g pork mince
- 180 ml bread crumbs
- 60 ml grated Parmesan cheese
- 60 ml finely chopped fresh parsley
- ½ teaspoon dried oregano
- 1½ teaspoons salt
- Freshly ground black pepper, to taste
- 2 eggs, lightly beaten
- 140 g low-moisture Mozzarella or other melting cheese, cut into 1-inch cubes

Directions:
1. Preheat a skillet over medium-high heat. Add the oil and cook the onion and garlic until tender, but not browned. 2. Transfer the onion and garlic to a large bowl and add the beef, pork, bread crumbs, Parmesan cheese, parsley, oregano, salt, pepper and eggs. Mix well until all the ingredients are combined. Divide the mixture into 12 evenly sized balls. Make one meatball at a time, by pressing a hole in the meatball mixture with the finger and pushing a piece of Mozzarella cheese into the hole. Mold the meat back into a ball, enclosing the cheese. 3. Preheat the air fryer to 192°C. 4. Transfer meatballs to the two air fryer drawers and air fry for 12 minutes, shaking the drawers and turning the meatballs twice during the cooking process. Serve warm.

Smothered Chops

Servings: 4
Cooking Time: 30 Minutes

Ingredients:

- 4 bone-in pork chops (230 g each)
- 2 teaspoons salt, divided
- 1½ teaspoons freshly ground black pepper, divided
- 1 teaspoon garlic powder
- 235 ml tomato purée
- 1½ teaspoons Italian seasoning
- 1 tablespoon sugar
- 1 tablespoon cornflour
- 120 ml chopped onion
- 120 ml chopped green pepper
- 1 to 2 tablespoons oil

Directions:

1. Evenly season the pork chops with 1 teaspoon salt, 1 teaspoon pepper, and the garlic powder.
2. In a medium bowl, stir together the tomato purée, Italian seasoning, sugar, remaining 1 teaspoon of salt, and remaining ½ teaspoon of pepper.
3. In a small bowl, whisk 180 ml water and the cornflour until blended. Stir this slurry into the tomato purée, with the onion and green pepper. Transfer to a baking pan.
4. Preheat the air fryer to 176°C.
5. Place the sauce in the fryer and cook for 10 minutes. Stir and cook for 10 minutes more. Remove the pan and keep warm.
6. Increase the air fryer temperature to 204°C. Line the two air fryer drawers with parchment paper.
7. Place the pork chops on the parchment and spritz with oil.
8. Cook for 5 minutes. Flip and spritz the chops with oil and cook for 5 minutes more, until the internal temperature reaches 64°C. Serve with the tomato mixture spooned on top.

Bacon Wrapped Pork Tenderloin

Servings: 2
Cooking Time: 20 Minutes

Ingredients:

- ½ teaspoon salt
- ¼ teaspoon black pepper
- 1 pork tenderloin
- 6 center cut strips bacon
- cooking string

Directions:

1. Cut two bacon strips in half and place them on the working surface.
2. Place the other bacon strips on top and lay the tenderloin over the bacon strip.
3. Wrap the bacon around the tenderloin and tie the roast with a kitchen string.
4. Place the roast in the first air fryer basket.
5. Return the air fryer basket 1 to Zone 1, and basket 2 to Zone 2 of the Ninja Foodi 2-Basket Air Fryer.
6. Choose the "Air Fry" mode for Zone 1 and set the temperature to 400 degrees F and 20 minutes of cooking time.
7. Initiate cooking by pressing the START/PAUSE BUTTON.
8. Slice and serve warm.

Italian Sausages With Peppers And Teriyaki Rump Steak With Broccoli

Servings: 7
Cooking Time: 28 Minutes

Ingredients:
- Italian Sausages with Peppers:
- 1 medium onion, thinly sliced
- 1 yellow or orange pepper, thinly sliced
- 1 red pepper, thinly sliced
- 60 ml avocado oil or melted coconut oil
- 1 teaspoon fine sea salt
- 6 Italian-seasoned sausages
- Dijon mustard, for serving (optional)
- Teriyaki Rump Steak with Broccoli:
- 230 g rump steak
- 80 ml teriyaki marinade
- 1½ teaspoons sesame oil
- ½ head broccoli, cut into florets
- 2 red peppers, sliced
- Fine sea salt and ground black pepper, to taste
- Cooking spray

Directions:
1. Make the Italian Sausages with Peppers :
2. Preheat the air fryer to 204°C.
3. Place the onion and peppers in a large bowl. Drizzle with the oil and toss well to coat the veggies. Season with the salt.
4. Place the onion and peppers in a pie pan and cook in the air fryer for 8 minutes, stirring halfway through. Remove from the air fryer and set aside.
5. Spray the zone 1 air fryer drawer with avocado oil. Place the sausages in the zone 1 air fryer drawer and air fry for 20 minutes, or until crispy and golden brown. During the last minute or two of cooking, add the onion and peppers to the drawer with the sausages to warm them through.
6. Place the onion and peppers on a serving platter and arrange the sausages on top. Serve Dijon mustard on the side, if desired.
7. Store leftovers in an airtight container in the fridge for up to 7 days or in the freezer for up to a month. Reheat in a preheated 200°C air fryer for 3 minutes, or until heated through.
8. Make the Teriyaki Rump Steak with Broccoli :
9. Toss the rump steak in a large bowl with teriyaki marinade. Wrap the bowl in plastic and refrigerate to marinate for at least an hour.
10. Preheat the air fryer to 204°C and spritz with cooking spray.
11. Discard the marinade and transfer the steak in the preheated zone 2 air fryer drawer. Spritz with cooking spray.
12. Air fry for 13 minutes or until well browned. Flip the steak halfway through.
13. Meanwhile, heat the sesame oil in a nonstick skillet over medium heat. Add the broccoli and red pepper. Sprinkle with salt and ground black pepper. Sauté for 5 minutes or until the broccoli is tender.
14. Transfer the air fried rump steak on a plate and top with the sautéed broccoli and pepper. Serve hot.

Spicy Lamb Chops

Servings: 4
Cooking Time: 15
Ingredients:
- 12 lamb chops, bone-in
- Salt and black pepper, to taste
- ½ teaspoon of lemon zest
- 1 tablespoon of lemon juice
- 1 teaspoon of paprika
- 1 teaspoon of garlic powder
- ½ teaspoon of Italian seasoning
- ¼ teaspoon of onion powder

Directions:
1. Add the lamb chops to the bowl and sprinkle salt, garlic powder, Italian seasoning, onion powder, black pepper, lemon zest, lemon juice, and paprika.
2. Rub the chops well, and divide it between both the baskets of the air fryer.
3. Set zone 1 basket to 400 degrees F, for 15 minutes at AIR FRY mode.
4. Select MATCH for zone2 basket.
5. After 10 minutes, take out the baskets and flip the chops cook for the remaining minutes, and then serve.

Nutrition:
- (Per serving) Calories 787| Fat 45.3g| Sodium1 mg | Carbs 16.1g | Fiber0.3g | Sugar 0.4g | Protein 75.3g

Steak Fajitas With Onions And Peppers

Servings: 6
Cooking Time: 15 Minutes
Ingredients:
- 1 pound steak
- 1 green bell pepper, sliced
- 1 yellow bell pepper, sliced
- 1 red bell pepper, sliced
- ½ cup sliced white onions
- 1 packet gluten-free fajita seasoning
- Olive oil spray

Directions:
1. Thinly slice the steak against the grain. These should be about ¼-inch slices.
2. Mix the steak with the peppers and onions.
3. Evenly coat with the fajita seasoning.
4. Install a crisper plate in both drawers. Place half the steak mixture in the zone 1 drawer and half in zone 2's, then insert the drawers into the unit.
5. Select zone 1, select AIR FRY, set temperature to 390 degrees F/ 200 degrees C, and set time to 15 minutes. Select MATCH to match zone 2 settings to zone 1. Press the START/STOP button to begin cooking.
6. When the time reaches 10 minutes, press START/STOP to pause the unit. Remove the drawers and flip the steak strips. Re-insert the drawers into the unit and press START/STOP to resume cooking.
7. Serve in warm tortillas.

Nutrition:
- (Per serving) Calories 305 | Fat 17g | Sodium 418mg | Carbs 15g | Fiber 2g | Sugar 4g | Protein 22g

Asian Glazed Meatballs

Servings: 4 To 6
Cooking Time: 10 Minutes
Ingredients:
- 1 large shallot, finely chopped
- 2 cloves garlic, minced
- 1 tablespoon grated fresh ginger
- 2 teaspoons fresh thyme, finely chopped
- 355 ml brown mushrooms, very finely chopped
- 2 tablespoons soy sauce
- Freshly ground black pepper, to taste
- 450 g beef mince
- 230 g pork mince
- 3 egg yolks
- 235 ml Thai sweet chili sauce (spring roll sauce)
- 60 ml toasted sesame seeds
- 2 spring onions, sliced

Directions:
1. Combine the shallot, garlic, ginger, thyme, mushrooms, soy sauce, freshly ground black pepper, beef and pork mince, and egg yolks in a bowl and mix the ingredients together. Gently shape the mixture into 24 balls, about the size of a golf ball.
2. Preheat the air fryer to 192°C.
3. Air fry the meatballs in the two drawers for 8 minutes, turning the meatballs over halfway through the cooking time. Drizzle some of the Thai sweet chili sauce on top of each meatball and return the drawers to the air fryer, air frying for another 2 minutes. Reserve the remaining Thai sweet chili sauce for serving.
4. As soon as the meatballs are done, sprinkle with toasted sesame seeds and transfer them to a serving platter. Scatter the spring onions around and serve warm.

Marinated Pork Chops

Servings: 2
Cooking Time: 12 Minutes
Ingredients:
- 2 pork chops, boneless
- 18g sugar
- 1 tbsp water
- 15ml rice wine
- 15ml dark soy sauce
- 15ml light soy sauce
- ½ tsp cinnamon
- ½ tsp five-spice powder
- 1 tsp black pepper

Directions:
1. Add pork chops and remaining ingredients into a zip-lock bag. Seal the bag and place in the refrigerator for 4 hours.
2. Insert a crisper plate in the Ninja Foodi air fryer baskets.
3. Place the marinated pork chops in both baskets.
4. Select zone 1, then select air fry mode and set the temperature to 380 degrees F for 12 minutes. Press "match" to match zone 2 settings to zone 1. Press "start/stop" to begin.

Parmesan Pork Chops

Servings: 4
Cooking Time: 15 Minutes.

Ingredients:
- 4 boneless pork chops
- 2 tablespoons olive oil
- ½ cup freshly grated Parmesan
- 1 teaspoon salt
- 1 teaspoon paprika
- 1 teaspoon garlic powder
- 1 teaspoon onion powder
- ½ teaspoon black pepper

Directions:
1. Pat dry the pork chops with a paper towel and rub them with olive oil.
2. Mix parmesan with spices in a medium bowl.
3. Rub the pork chops with Parmesan mixture.
4. Place 2 seasoned pork chops in each of the two crisper plate
5. Return the crisper plate to the Ninja Foodi Dual Zone Air Fryer.
6. Choose the Air Fry mode for Zone 1 and set the temperature to 390 degrees F and the time to 15 minutes.
7. Select the "MATCH" button to copy the settings for Zone 2.
8. Initiate cooking by pressing the START/STOP button.
9. Flip the pork chops when cooked halfway through, then resume cooking.
10. Serve warm.

Nutrition:
- (Per serving) Calories 396 | Fat 23.2g |Sodium 622mg | Carbs 0.7g | Fiber 0g | Sugar 0g | Protein 45.6g

Roast Beef

Servings: 4
Cooking Time: 35 Minutes

Ingredients:
- 2 pounds beef roast
- 1 tablespoon olive oil
- 1 medium onion (optional)
- 1 teaspoon salt
- 2 teaspoons rosemary and thyme, chopped (fresh or dried)

Directions:
1. Combine the sea salt, rosemary, and oil in a large, shallow dish.
2. Using paper towels, pat the meat dry. Place it on a dish and turn it to coat the outside with the oil-herb mixture.
3. Peel the onion and split it in half (if using).
4. Install a crisper plate in both drawers. Place half the beef roast and half an onion in the zone 1 drawer and half the beef and half the onion in zone 2's, then insert the drawers into the unit.
5. Select zone 1, select AIR FRY, set temperature to 360 degrees F/ 180 degrees C, and set time to 22 minutes. Select MATCH to match zone 2 settings to zone 1. Press the START/STOP button to begin cooking.
6. When the time reaches 11 minutes, press START/STOP to pause the unit. Remove the drawers and flip the roast. Re-insert the drawers into the unit and press START/STOP to resume cooking.

Nutrition:
- (Per serving) Calories 463 | Fat 17.8g | Sodium 732mg | Carbs 2.8g | Fiber 0.7g | Sugar 1.2g | Protein 69g

Ham Burger Patties

Servings: 2
Cooking Time: 17

Ingredients:

- 1 pound of ground beef
- Salt and pepper, to taste
- ½ teaspoon of red chili powder
- ¼ teaspoon of coriander powder
- 2 tablespoons of chopped onion
- 1 green chili, chopped
- Oil spray for greasing
- 2 large potato wedges

Directions:

1. Oil greases the air fryer baskets with oil spray.
2. Add potato wedges in the zone 1 basket.
3. Take a bowl and add minced beef in it and add salt, pepper, chili powder, coriander powder, green chili, and chopped onion.
4. mix well and make two burger patties with wet hands place the two patties in the air fryer zone 2 basket.
5. put the basket inside the air fryer.
6. now, set time for zone 1 for 12 minutes using AIR FRY mode at 400 degrees F.
7. Select the MATCH button for zone 2.
8. once the time of cooking complete, take out the baskets.
9. flip the patties and shake the potatoes wedges.
10. again, set time of zone 1 basket for 4 minutes at 400 degrees F
11. Select the MATCH button for the second basket.
12. Once it's done, serve and enjoy.

Nutrition:

- (Per serving) Calories875 | Fat21.5g | Sodium 622mg | Carbs 88g | Fiber10.9 g| Sugar 3.4g | Protein 78.8g

Steak In Air Fry

Servings: 1
Cooking Time: 20

Ingredients:

- 2 teaspoons of canola oil
- 1 tablespoon of Montreal steaks seasoning
- 1 pound of beef steak

Directions:

1. The first step is to season the steak on both sides with canola oil and then rub a generous amount of steak seasoning all over.
2. We are using the AIR BROIL feature of the ninja air fryer and it works with one basket.
3. Put the steak in the basket and set it to AIR BROIL at 450 degrees F for 20 -22 minutes.
4. After 7 minutes, hit pause and take out the basket to flip the steak, and cover it with foil on top, for the remaining 14 minutes.
5. Once done, serve the medium-rare steak and enjoy it by resting for 10 minutes.
6. Serve by cutting in slices.
7. Enjoy.

Nutrition:

- (Per serving) Calories 935| Fat 37.2g| Sodium 1419mg | Carbs 0g | Fiber 0g| Sugar 0g | Protein137.5 g

Pork With Green Beans And Potatoes

Servings: 4
Cooking Time: 15 Minutes.
Ingredients:
- ¼ cup Dijon mustard
- 2 tablespoons brown sugar
- 1 teaspoon dried parsley flake
- ½ teaspoon dried thyme
- ¼ teaspoons salt
- ¼ teaspoons black pepper
- 1 ¼ lbs. pork tenderloin
- ¾ lb. small potatoes halved
- 1 (12-oz) package green beans, trimmed
- 1 tablespoon olive oil
- Salt and black pepper ground to taste

Directions:
1. Preheat your Air Fryer Machine to 400 degrees F.
2. Add mustard, parsley, brown sugar, salt, black pepper, and thyme in a large bowl, then mix well.
3. Add tenderloin to the spice mixture and coat well.
4. Toss potatoes with olive oil, salt, black pepper, and green beans in another bowl.
5. Place the prepared tenderloin in the crisper plate.
6. Return this crisper plate to the Zone 1 of the Ninja Foodi Dual Zone Air Fryer.
7. Choose the Air Fry mode for Zone 1 and set the temperature to 390 degrees F and the time to 15 minutes.
8. Add potatoes and green beans to the Zone 2.
9. Choose the Air Fry mode for Zone 2 with 350 degrees F and the time to 10 minutes.
10. Press the SYNC button to sync the finish time for both Zones.
11. Initiate cooking by pressing the START/STOP button.
12. Serve the tenderloin with Air Fried potatoes

Nutrition:
- (Per serving) Calories 400 | Fat 32g |Sodium 721mg | Carbs 2.6g | Fiber 0g | Sugar 0g | Protein 27.4g

Snacks And Appetizers Recipes

Fried Cheese

Servings: 4
Cooking Time: 15 Minutes
Ingredients:
- 1 Mozzarella cheese block, cut into sticks
- 2 teaspoons olive oil

Directions:
1. Divide the cheese slices into the Ninja Foodi 2 Baskets Air Fryer baskets.
2. Drizzle olive oil over the cheese slices.
3. Return the air fryer basket 1 to Zone 1, and basket 2 to Zone 2 of the Ninja Foodi 2-Basket Air Fryer.
4. Choose the "Air Fry" mode for Zone 1 and set the temperature to 360 degrees F and 12 minutes of cooking time.
5. Flip the cheese slices once cooked halfway through.
6. Serve.

Pretzels Hot Dog

Servings: 8
Cooking Time: 15 Minutes

Ingredients:
- 180ml warm water
- 2¼ teaspoons instant yeast
- 1 teaspoon sugar
- 2 teaspoons olive oil
- 250g plain flour
- ½ teaspoon salt
- 1 large egg
- 1 tablespoon water
- 8 hot dogs

Directions:
1. Combine warm water, yeast, sugar, and olive oil in a large mixing basin to make the dough.
2. Stir everything together and leave aside for about 5 minutes.
3. Mix in roughly 125g flour and a pinch of salt. Add 125g of flour at a time until the dough comes together into a ball and pulls away from the bowl's sides.
4. On a floured board, pour the dough. Knead the dough for 3 to 5 minutes, adding extra flour until it is no longer sticky.
5. Cut the dough into eight pieces.
6. Roll the dough between your hands, and roll each piece into an 20 cm to 25 cm rope.
7. Pat, the hot dogs, dry with paper towels to make wrapping the dough around them easier.
8. Begin wrapping the dough around one end of each hot dog in a spiral. To seal the ends, pinch them together.
9. In a small mixing dish, whisk together an egg and a tablespoon of water. Coat the dough in egg wash from all sides.
10. Press your chosen zone - "Zone 1" or "Zone 2" and then rotate the knob to select "Air Fryer".
11. Set the temperature to 200 degrees C, and then set the time for 5 minutes to preheat.
12. After preheating, arrange pretzels into the basket of each zone.
13. Slide the baskets into Air Fryer and set the time for 8 minutes.
14. After cooking time is completed, place on a wire rack for a few minutes, then transfer onto serving plates and serve.

Waffle Fries

Servings: 2
Cooking Time: 15 Minutes

Ingredients:
- 2 russet potatoes
- ½ teaspoon seasoning salt

Directions:
1. If desired, peel the potatoes.
2. With Wave-Waffle Cutter, slice potatoes by turning them one-quarter turn after each pass over the blade.
3. In a mixing dish, toss the potato pieces with the seasoning salt. Toss the potatoes in the seasoning to ensure that it is uniformly distributed.
4. Place a baking sheet on the baskets.
5. Press either "Zone 1" or "Zone 2" and then rotate the knob to select "Air Fryer".
6. Set the temperature to 200 degrees C, and then set the time for 5 minutes to preheat.
7. After preheating, arrange them into the basket.
8. Slide the basket into the Air Fryer and set the time for 15 minutes.
9. After cooking time is completed, place on a wire rack for a few minutes, then transfer onto serving plates and serve.

Potato Chips

Servings: 4
Cooking Time: 15 Minutes

Ingredients:
- 2 large potatoes, peeled and sliced
- 1½ teaspoons salt
- 1½ teaspoons black pepper
- Oil for misting

Directions:
1. Soak potatoes in cold water for 30 minutes then drain.
2. Pat dry the potato slices and toss them with cracked pepper, salt and oil mist.
3. Spread the potatoes in the air fryer basket.
4. Return the air fryer basket 1 to Zone 1, and basket 2 to Zone 2 of the Ninja Foodi 2-Basket Air Fryer.
5. Choose the "Air Fry" mode for Zone 1 at 300 degrees F and 16 minutes of cooking time.
6. Select the "MATCH COOK" option to copy the settings for Zone 2.
7. Initiate cooking by pressing the START/PAUSE BUTTON.
8. Toss the fries once cooked halfway through.
9. Serve warm.

Strawberries And Walnuts Muffins

Servings: 2
Cooking Time: 15

Ingredients:
- Salt, pinch
- 2 eggs, whisked
- 1/3 cup maple syrup
- 1/3 cup coconut oil
- 4 tablespoons of water
- 1 teaspoon of orange zest
- ¼ teaspoon of vanilla extract
- ½ teaspoon of baking powder
- 1 cup all-purpose flour
- 1 cup strawberries, finely chopped
- 1/3 cup walnuts, chopped and roasted

Directions:
1. Take one cup size of 4 ramekins that are oven safe.
2. Layer it with muffin paper.
3. In a bowl and add egg, maple syrup, oil, water, vanilla extract, and orange zest.
4. Whisk it all very well
5. In a separate bowl, mix flour, baking powder, and salt.
6. Now add dry ingredients slowly to wet ingredients.
7. Now pour this batter into ramekins and top it with strawberries and walnuts.
8. Now divide it between both zones and set the time for zone 1 basket to 15 minutes at 350 degrees F.
9. Select the MATCH button for the zone 2 basket.
10. Check if not done let it AIR FRY FOR one more minute.
11. Once done, serve.

Nutrition:
- (Per serving) Calories 897| Fat 53.9g | Sodium 148mg | Carbs 92g | Fiber 4.7g| Sugar 35.6 g | Protein 17.5g

Zucchini Chips

Servings: 4
Cooking Time: 15 Minutes
Ingredients:
- 1 medium-sized zucchini
- ½ cup panko breadcrumbs
- ½ teaspoon garlic powder
- ¼ teaspoon onion powder
- 1 egg
- 3 tablespoons flour

Directions:
1. Slice the zucchini into thin slices, about ¼-inch thick.
2. In a mixing bowl, combine the panko breadcrumbs, garlic powder, and onion powder.
3. The egg should be whisked in a different bowl, while the flour should be placed in a third bowl.
4. Dip the zucchini slices in the flour, then in the egg, and finally in the breadcrumbs.
5. Place a crisper plate in each drawer. Put the zucchini slices into each drawer in a single layer. Insert the drawers into the unit.
6. Select zone 1, then AIR FRY, then set the temperature to 360 degrees F/ 180 degrees C with a 6-minute timer. To match zone 2 settings to zone 1, choose MATCH. To begin, select START/STOP.
7. Remove the zucchini from the drawers after the timer has finished.

Nutrition:
- (Per serving) Calories 82 | Fat 1.5g | Sodium 89mg | Carbs 14.1g | Fiber 1.7g | Sugar 1.2g | Protein 3.9g

Beef Skewers

Servings: 6
Cooking Time: 5 Minutes
Ingredients:
- 1 beef flank steak
- 240ml rice vinegar
- 240ml soy sauce
- 55g packed brown sugar
- 2 tablespoons minced fresh gingerroot
- 6 garlic cloves, minced
- 3 teaspoons sesame oil
- 1 teaspoon hot pepper sauce
- ½ teaspoon cornflour

Directions:
1. Cut beef into ½ cm thick strips. Whisk together the following 7 ingredients in a large mixing bowl until well combined.
2. In a shallow dish, pour 1 cup of marinade. Toss in the beef and turn to coat. Refrigerate for 2-8 hours, covered. Cover and keep the remaining marinade refrigerated.
3. Beef should be drained. 12 metal or wet wooden skewers threaded with beef.
4. Press either "Zone 1" or "Zone 2" and then rotate the knob to select "Air Fry".
5. Set the temperature to 200 degrees C, and then set the time for 5 minutes to preheat.
6. After preheating, spray the basket with cooking spray and arrange skewers onto basket.
7. Slide the basket into the Air Fryer and set the time for 5 minutes.
8. After cooking time is completed, transfer them onto serving plates and serve.

Cheese Stuffed Mushrooms

Servings: 4
Cooking Time: 10 Minutes
Ingredients:
- 176g button mushrooms, clean & cut stems
- 46g sour cream
- 17g cream cheese, softened
- ½ tsp garlic powder
- 58g cheddar cheese, shredded
- Pepper
- Salt

Directions:
1. In a small bowl, mix cream cheese, garlic powder, sour cream, pepper, and salt.
2. Stuff cream cheese mixture into each mushroom and top each with cheddar cheese.
3. Insert a crisper plate in the Ninja Foodi air fryer baskets.
4. Place the stuffed mushrooms in both baskets.
5. Select zone 1 then select "air fry" mode and set the temperature to 370 degrees F for 8 minutes. Press "match" to match zone 2 settings to zone 1. Press "start/stop" to begin.

Chicken Crescent Wraps

Servings: 6
Cooking Time: 12 Minutes.
Ingredients:
- 3 tablespoons chopped onion
- 3 garlic cloves, peeled and minced
- ¾ (8 ounces) package cream cheese
- 6 tablespoons butter
- 2 boneless chicken breasts, cubed, cooked
- 3 (10 ounces) cans refrigerated crescent roll dough

Directions:
1. Heat oil in a skillet and add onion and garlic to sauté until soft.
2. Add cooked chicken, sautéed veggies, butter, and cream cheese to a blender.
3. Blend well until smooth. Spread the crescent dough over a flat surface.
4. Slice the dough into 12 rectangles.
5. Spoon the chicken mixture at the center of each rectangle.
6. Roll the dough to wrap the mixture and form a ball.
7. Divide these balls into the two crisper plate.
8. Return the crisper plate to the Ninja Foodi Dual Zone Air Fryer.
9. Choose the Air Fry mode for Zone 1 and set the temperature to 390 degrees F and the time to 12 minutes.
10. Select the "MATCH" button to copy the settings for Zone 2.
11. Initiate cooking by pressing the START/STOP button.
12. Serve warm.

Nutrition:
- (Per serving) Calories 100 | Fat 2g | Sodium 480mg | Carbs 4g | Fiber 2g | Sugar 0g | Protein 18g

Healthy Spinach Balls

Servings: 4
Cooking Time: 15 Minutes

Ingredients:
- 1 egg
- 29g breadcrumbs
- ½ medium onion, chopped
- 225g spinach, blanched & chopped
- 1 carrot, peel & grated
- 1 tbsp cornflour
- 1 tbsp nutritional yeast
- 1 tsp garlic, minced
- ½ tsp garlic powder
- Pepper
- Salt

Directions:
1. Add spinach and remaining ingredients into the mixing bowl and mix until well combined.
2. Insert a crisper plate in the Ninja Foodi air fryer baskets.
3. Make small balls from the spinach mixture and place them in both baskets.
4. Select zone 1, then select "air fry" mode and set the temperature to 390 degrees F for 10 minutes. Press "match" to match zone 2 settings to zone 1. Press "start/stop" to begin.

Jalapeño Popper Chicken

Servings: 4
Cooking Time: 50 Minutes

Ingredients:
- 2 ounces cream cheese, softened
- ¼ cup shredded cheddar cheese
- ¼ cup shredded mozzarella cheese
- ¼ teaspoon garlic powder
- 4 small jalapeño peppers, seeds removed and diced
- Kosher salt, as desired
- Ground black pepper, as desired
- 4 organic boneless, skinless chicken breasts
- 8 slices bacon

Directions:
1. Cream together the cream cheese, cheddar cheese, mozzarella cheese, garlic powder, and jalapeño in a mixing bowl. Add salt and pepper to taste.
2. Make a deep pocket in the center of each chicken breast, but be cautious not to cut all the way through.
3. Fill each chicken breast's pocket with the cream cheese mixture.
4. Wrap two strips of bacon around each chicken breast and attach them with toothpicks.
5. Place a crisper plate in each drawer. Put the chicken breasts in the drawers. Place both drawers in the unit.
6. Select zone 1, then AIR FRY, and set the temperature to 350 degrees F/ 175 degrees C with a 30-minute timer. To match zone 2 and zone 1 settings, select MATCH. To begin cooking, press the START/STOP button.
7. When cooking is complete, remove the chicken breasts and allow them to rest for 5 minutes before serving

Nutrition:
- (Per serving) Calories 507 | Fat 27.5g | Sodium 1432mg | Carbs 2.3g | Fiber 0.6g | Sugar 0.6g | Protein 58.2g

Beef Jerky Pineapple Jerky

Servings: 8
Cooking Time: 6 To 12 Hours
Ingredients:
- FOR THE BEEF JERKY
- ½ cup reduced-sodium soy sauce
- ¼ cup pineapple juice
- 1 tablespoon dark brown sugar
- 1 tablespoon Worcestershire sauce
- ½ teaspoon smoked paprika
- ¼ teaspoon freshly ground black pepper
- ¼ teaspoon red pepper flakes
- 1 pound beef bottom round, trimmed of excess fat, cut into ¼-inch-thick slices
- FOR THE PINEAPPLE JERKY
- 1 pound pineapple, cut into ⅛-inch-thick rounds, pat dry
- 1 teaspoon chili powder (optional)

Directions:
1. To prep the beef jerky: In a large zip-top bag, combine the soy sauce, pineapple juice, brown sugar, Worcestershire sauce, smoked paprika, black pepper, and red pepper flakes.
2. Add the beef slices, seal the bag, and toss to coat the meat in the marinade. Refrigerate overnight or for at least 8 hours.
3. Remove the beef slices and discard the marinade. Using a paper towel, pat the slices dry to remove excess marinade.
4. To prep the pineapple jerky: Sprinkle the pineapple with chili powder (if using).
5. To dehydrate the jerky: Arrange half of the beef slices in a single layer in the Zone 1 basket, making sure they do not overlap. Place a crisper plate on top of the beef slices and arrange the remaining slices in a single layer on top of the crisper plate. Insert the basket in the unit.
6. Repeat this process with the pineapple in the Zone 2 basket and insert the basket in the unit.
7. Select Zone 1, select DEHYDRATE, set the temperature to 150°F, and set the time to 8 hours.
8. Select Zone 2, select DEHYDRATE, set the temperature to 135°F, and set the time to 12 hours.
9. Press START/PAUSE to begin cooking.
10. When the Zone 1 timer reads 2 hours, press START/PAUSE. Remove the basket and check the beef jerky for doneness. If necessary, reinsert the basket and press START/PAUSE to resume cooking.

Nutrition:
- (Per serving) Calories: 171; Total fat: 6.5g; Saturated fat: 2g; Carbohydrates: 2g; Fiber: 0g; Protein: 25g; Sodium: 369mg

Crispy Filo Artichoke Triangles

Servings: 18 Triangles
Cooking Time: 9 To 12 Minutes
Ingredients:
- 60 ml Ricotta cheese
- 1 egg white
- 80 ml minced and drained artichoke hearts
- 3 tablespoons grated Mozzarella cheese
- ½ teaspoon dried thyme
- 6 sheets frozen filo pastry, thawed
- 2 tablespoons melted butter

Directions:
1. Preheat the air fryer to 205°C.

2. In a small bowl, combine the Ricotta cheese, egg white, artichoke hearts, Mozzarella cheese, and thyme, and mix well.
3. Cover the filo pastry with a damp kitchen towel while you work so it doesn't dry out. Using one sheet at a time, place on the work surface and cut into thirds lengthwise.
4. Put about 1½ teaspoons of the filling on each strip at the base. Fold the bottom right-hand tip of phyllo over the filling to meet the other side in a triangle, then continue folding in a triangle. Brush each triangle with butter to seal the edges. Repeat with the remaining phyllo dough and filling.
5. Place the triangles in the two air fryer baskets. Bake, 6 at a time, in two baskets for about 3 to 4 minutes, or until the filo is golden brown and crisp.
6. Serve hot.

Taco-spiced Chickpeas And Black Bean Corn Dip

Servings: 7
Cooking Time: 17 Minutes
Ingredients:
- Taco-Spiced Chickpeas:
- Oil, for spraying
- 1 (439 g) can chickpeas, drained
- 1 teaspoon chilli powder
- ½ teaspoon ground cumin
- ½ teaspoon salt
- ½ teaspoon granulated garlic
- 2 teaspoons lime juice
- Black Bean Corn Dip:
- ½ (425 g) can black beans, drained and rinsed
- ½ (425 g) can corn, drained and rinsed
- 60 ml chunky salsa
- 57 g low-fat soft white cheese
- 60 ml shredded low-fat Cheddar cheese
- ½ teaspoon ground cumin
- ½ teaspoon paprika
- Salt and freshly ground black pepper, to taste

Directions:
1. Make the Taco-Spiced Chickpeas :
2. Line the zone 1 air fryer basket with parchment and spray lightly with oil. Place the chickpeas in the prepared basket.
3. Air fry at 200°C for 17 minutes, shaking or stirring the chickpeas and spraying lightly with oil every 5 to 7 minutes.
4. In a small bowl, mix together the chilli powder, cumin, salt, and garlic.
5. When 2 to 3 minutes of cooking time remain, sprinkle half of the seasoning mix over the chickpeas. Finish cooking.
6. Transfer the chickpeas to a medium bowl and toss with the remaining seasoning mix and the lime juice. Serve immediately.
7. Make the Black Bean Corn Dip :
8. Preheat the air fryer to 165°C.
9. In a medium bowl, mix together the black beans, corn, salsa, soft white cheese, Cheddar cheese, cumin, and paprika. Season with salt and pepper and stir until well combined.
10. Spoon the mixture into a baking dish.
11. Place baking dish in the zone 2 air fryer basket and bake until heated through, about 10 minutes.
12. Serve hot.

Chicken Stuffed Mushrooms

Servings: 6
Cooking Time: 15 Minutes.
Ingredients:
- 6 large fresh mushrooms, stems removed
- Stuffing:
- ½ cup chicken meat, cubed
- 1 (4 ounces) package cream cheese, softened
- ¼ lb. imitation crabmeat, flaked
- 1 cup butter
- 1 garlic clove, peeled and minced
- Black pepper and salt to taste
- Garlic powder to taste
- Crushed red pepper to taste

Directions:
1. Melt and heat butter in a skillet over medium heat.
2. Add chicken and sauté for 5 minutes.
3. Add in all the remaining ingredients for the stuffing.
4. Cook for 5 minutes, then turn off the heat.
5. Allow the mixture to cool. Stuff each mushroom with a tablespoon of this mixture.
6. Divide the stuffed mushrooms in the two crisper plates.
7. Return the crisper plate to the Ninja Foodi Dual Zone Air Fryer.
8. Choose the Air Fry mode for Zone 1 and set the temperature to 375 degrees F and the time to 15 minutes.
9. Select the "MATCH" button to copy the settings for Zone 2.
10. Initiate cooking by pressing the START/STOP button.
11. Serve warm.

Nutrition:
- (Per serving) Calories 180 | Fat 3.2g |Sodium 133mg | Carbs 32g | Fiber 1.1g | Sugar 1.8g | Protein 9g

Cheese Corn Fritters

Servings: 6
Cooking Time: 15 Minutes
Ingredients:
- 1 egg
- 164g corn
- 2 green onions, diced
- 45g flour
- 29g breadcrumbs
- 117g cheddar cheese, shredded
- ½ tsp onion powder
- ½ tsp garlic powder
- 15g sour cream
- Pepper
- Salt

Directions:
1. In a large bowl, add all ingredients and mix until well combined.
2. Insert a crisper plate in the Ninja Foodi air fryer baskets.
3. Make patties from the mixture and place them in both baskets.
4. Select zone 1, then select "air fry" mode and set the temperature to 370 degrees F for 12 minutes. Press "match" to match zone 2 settings to zone 1. Press "start/stop" to begin. Turn halfway through.

Mexican Jalapeno Poppers

Servings: 8
Cooking Time: 5 Minutes
Ingredients:
- 5 jalapenos, cut in half & remove seeds
- ¼ tsp red pepper flakes, crushed
- 1 tsp onion powder
- 32g salsa
- 113g goat cheese
- 1 tsp garlic powder
- Pepper
- Salt

Directions:
1. In a small bowl, mix goat cheese, salsa, red pepper flakes, onion powder, garlic powder, pepper, and salt.
2. Stuff each jalapeno half with goat cheese mixture.
3. Insert a crisper plate in the Ninja Foodi air fryer baskets.
4. Place stuffed peppers in both baskets.
5. Select zone 1 then select "air fry" mode and set the temperature to 360 degrees F for 8 minutes—Press "match" to match zone 2 settings to zone 1. Press "start/stop" to begin.

Crab Cake Poppers

Servings: 6
Cooking Time: 15 Minutes
Ingredients:
- 1 egg, lightly beaten
- 453g lump crab meat, drained
- 1 tsp garlic, minced
- 1 tsp lemon juice
- 1 tsp old bay seasoning
- 30g almond flour
- 1 tsp Dijon mustard
- 28g mayonnaise
- Pepper
- Salt

Dirctions:
1. In a bowl, mix crab meat and remaining ingredients until well combined.
2. Make small balls from the crab meat mixture and place them on a plate.
3. Place the plate in the refrigerator for 50 minutes.
4. Insert a crisper plate in the Ninja Foodi air fryer baskets.
5. Place the prepared crab meatballs in both baskets.
6. Select zone 1 then select "air fry" mode and set the temperature to 360 degrees F for 10 minutes. Press "match" to match zone 2 settings to zone 1. Press "start/stop" to begin.

Healthy Chickpea Fritters

Servings: 6
Cooking Time: 5 Minutes

Ingredients:
- 1 egg
- 425g can chickpeas, rinsed & drained
- ½ tsp ground ginger
- ½ tsp garlic powder
- 1 tsp ground cumin
- 2 green onions, sliced
- 15g fresh cilantro, chopped
- ½ tsp baking soda
- ½ tsp salt

Directions:
1. Add chickpeas and remaining ingredients into the food processor and process until well combined.
2. Insert a crisper plate in the Ninja Foodi air fryer baskets.
3. Make patties from the mixture and place them in both baskets.
4. Select zone 1, then select "air fry" mode and set the temperature to 390 degrees F for 5 minutes. Press "match" to match zone 2 settings to zone 1. Press "start/stop" to begin.

Caramelized Onion Dip With White Cheese

Servings: 8 To 10
Cooking Time: 30 Minutes

Ingredients:
- 1 tablespoon butter
- 1 medium onion, halved and thinly sliced
- ¼ teaspoon rock salt, plus additional for seasoning
- 113 g soft white cheese
- 120 ml sour cream
- ¼ teaspoon onion powder
- 1 tablespoon chopped fresh chives
- Black pepper, to taste
- Thick-cut potato crisps or vegetable crisps

Directions:
1. Place the butter in a baking pan. Place the pan in the zone 1 air fryer basket. Set the air fryer to 90°C for 1 minute, or until the butter is melted. Add the onions and salt to the pan.
2. Set the air fryer to 90°C for 15 minutes, or until onions are softened. Set the air fryer to 190°C for 15 minutes, until onions are a deep golden brown, stirring two or three times during the cooking time. Let cool completely.
3. In a medium bowl, stir together the cooked onions, soft white cheese, sour cream, onion powder, and chives. Season with salt and pepper. Cover and refrigerate for 2 hours to allow the flavours to blend.
4. Serve the dip with potato crisps or vegetable crisps.

Desserts Recipes

Sweet Potato Donut Holes

Servings: 18 Donut Holes
Cooking Time: 4 To 5 Minutes
Ingredients:
- 125 g plain flour
- 65 g granulated sugar
- ¼ teaspoon baking soda
- 1 teaspoon baking powder
- ⅛ teaspoon salt
- 125 g cooked & mashed purple sweet potatoes
- 1 egg, beaten
- 2 tablespoons butter, melted
- 1 teaspoon pure vanilla extract
- Coconut, or avocado oil for misting or cooking spray

Directions:
1. Preheat the air fryer to 200°C.
2. In a large bowl, stir together the flour, sugar, baking soda, baking powder, and salt.
3. In a separate bowl, combine the potatoes, egg, butter, and vanilla and mix well.
4. Add potato mixture to dry ingredients and stir into a soft dough.
5. Shape dough into 1½-inch balls. Mist lightly with oil or cooking spray.
6. Place the donut holes in the two air fryer baskets, leaving a little space in between. Cook for 4 to 5 minutes, until done in center and lightly browned outside.

Delicious Apple Fritters

Servings: 10
Cooking Time: 8 Minutes
Ingredients:
- 236g Bisquick
- 2 apples, peel & dice
- 158ml milk
- 30ml butter, melted
- 1 tsp cinnamon
- 24g sugar

Directions:
1. In a bowl, mix Bisquick, cinnamon, and sugar.
2. Add milk and mix until dough forms. Add apple and stir well.
3. Insert a crisper plate in Ninja Foodi air fryer baskets.
4. Make fritters from the mixture and place in both baskets. Brush fritters with melted butter.
5. Select zone 1 then select "air fry" mode and set the temperature to 360 degrees F for 10 minutes. Press "match" to match zone 2 settings to zone 1. Press "start/stop" to begin.

Nutrition:
- (Per serving) Calories 171 | Fat 6.7g | Sodium 352mg | Carbs 25.8g | Fiber 1.7g | Sugar 10.8g | Protein 2.7g

Chocó Lava Cake

Servings: 4
Cooking Time: 10 Minutes
Ingredients:
- 3 eggs
- 3 egg yolks
- 70g dark chocolate, chopped
- 168g cups powdered sugar
- 96g all-purpose flour
- 1 tsp vanilla
- 113g butter
- ½ tsp salt

Directions:
1. Add chocolate and butter to a bowl and microwave for 30 seconds. Remove from oven and stir until smooth.
2. Add eggs, egg yolks, sugar, flour, vanilla, and salt into the melted chocolate and stir until well combined.
3. Pour batter into the four greased ramekins.
4. Insert a crisper plate in Ninja Foodi air fryer baskets.
5. Place ramekins in both baskets.
6. Select zone 1 then select "air fry" mode and set the temperature to 390 degrees F for 10 minutes. Press "match" to match zone 2 settings to zone 1. Press "start/stop" to begin.

Nutrition:
- (Per serving) Calories 687 | Fat 37.3g | Sodium 527mg | Carbs 78.3g | Fiber 1.5g | Sugar 57.4g | Protein 10.7g

Apple Crumble

Servings: 4
Cooking Time: 30 Minutes
Ingredients:
- 1 can apple pie filling
- 6 tablespoons caster sugar
- 8 tablespoons self-rising flour
- ¼ cup butter, softened
- A pinch of salt

Directions:
1. Take a baking dish.
2. Arrange apple pie filling evenly into the prepared baking dish.
3. Take a large bowl, add all the remaining ingredients. Mix well.
4. Place the mixture evenly all over apple pie filling.
5. Press "Zone 1" and "Zone 2" and then rotate the knob for each zone to select "Bake".
6. Set the temperature to 320 degrees F/ 160 degrees C for both zones and then set the time for 5 minutes to preheat.
7. After preheating, arrange the baking dish into the basket of each zone.
8. Slide each basket into Air Fryer and set the time for 25 minutes.
9. After cooking time is completed, remove the baking dish from Air Fryer.
10. Set aside to cool.
11. Serve and enjoy!

Berry Crumble And S'mores

Servings: 8
Cooking Time: 15 Minutes
Ingredients:
- Berry Crumble:
- For the Filling:
- 300 g mixed berries
- 2 tablespoons sugar
- 1 tablespoon cornflour
- 1 tablespoon fresh lemon juice
- For the Topping:
- 30 g plain flour
- 20 g rolled oats
- 1 tablespoon granulated sugar
- 2 tablespoons cold unsalted butter, cut into small cubes
- Whipped cream or ice cream (optional)
- S'mores:
- Coconut, or avocado oil, for spraying
- 8 digestive biscuits
- 2 (45 g) chocolate bars
- 4 large marshmallows

Directions:
1. Make the Berry Crumble :
2. 1. Preheat the air fryer to 204°C. For the filling: In a round baking pan, gently mix the berries, sugar, cornflour, and lemon juice until thoroughly combined. 3. For the topping: In a small bowl, combine the flour, oats, and sugar. Stir the butter into the flour mixture until the mixture has the consistency of breadcrumbs. 4. Sprinkle the topping over the berries. 5. Put the pan in the zone 1 air fryer drawer and air fry for 15 minutes. Let cool for 5 minutes on a wire rack. 6. Serve topped with whipped cream or ice cream, if desired.
3. Make the S'mores :
4. Line the zone 2 air fryer drawer with baking paper and spray lightly with oil.
5. Place 4 biscuits into the prepared drawer.
6. Break the chocolate bars in half, and place 1/2 on top of each biscuit. Top with 1 marshmallow.
7. Air fry at 188°C for 30 seconds, or until the marshmallows are puffed, golden brown and slightly melted.
8. Top with the remaining biscuits and serve.

Air Fried Bananas

Servings: 4
Cooking Time: 15 Minutes
Ingredients:
- 4 bananas, sliced
- 1 avocado oil cooking spray

Directions:
1. Spread the banana slices in the two crisper plates in a single layer.
2. Drizzle avocado oil over the banana slices.
3. Return the crisper plate to the Ninja Foodi Dual Zone Air Fryer.
4. Choose the Air Fry mode for Zone 1 and set the temperature to 350 degrees F and the time to 13 minutes.
5. Select the "MATCH" button to copy the settings for Zone 2.
6. Initiate cooking by pressing the START/STOP button.
7. Serve.

Mini Blueberry Pies

Servings: 2
Cooking Time: 15 Minutes
Ingredients:
- 1 box store-bought pie dough, Trader Joe's
- ¼ cup blueberry jam
- 1 teaspoon lemon zest
- 1 egg white, for brushing

Directions:
1. Take the store-bought pie dough and cut it into 3-inch circles.
2. Brush the dough with egg white all around the edges.
3. Now add blueberry jam and zest in the middle and top it with another circle.
4. Press the edges with a fork to seal it.
5. Make a slit in the middle of each pie and divide them between the baskets.
6. Set zone 1 to AIR FRY mode 360 degrees for 10 minutes.
7. Select the MATCH button for zone 2.
8. Once cooked, serve.

Pecan Brownies And Cinnamon-sugar Almonds

Servings: 10
Cooking Time: 20 Minutes
Ingredients:
- Pecan Brownies:
- 50 g blanched finely ground almond flour
- 55 g powdered sweetener
- 2 tablespoons unsweetened cocoa powder
- ½ teaspoon baking powder
- 55 g unsalted butter, softened
- 1 large egg
- 35 g chopped pecans
- 40 g low-carb, sugar-free chocolate chips
- Cinnamon-Sugar Almonds:
- 150 g whole almonds
- 2 tablespoons salted butter, melted
- 1 tablespoon granulated sugar
- ½ teaspoon ground cinnamon

Directions:
1. Make the Pecan Brownies :
2. In a large bowl, mix almond flour, sweetener, cocoa powder, and baking powder. Stir in butter and egg.
3. Fold in pecans and chocolate chips. Scoop mixture into a round baking pan. Place pan into the zone 1 air fryer basket.
4. Adjust the temperature to 150°C and bake for 20 minutes.
5. When fully cooked a toothpick inserted in center will come out clean. Allow 20 minutes to fully cool and firm up.
6. Make the Cinnamon-Sugar Almonds :
7. In a medium bowl, combine the almonds, butter, sugar, and cinnamon. Mix well to ensure all the almonds are coated with the spiced butter.
8. Transfer the almonds to the zone 2 air fryer basket and shake so they are in a single layer. Set the air fryer to 150°C, and cook for 8 minutes, stirring the almonds halfway through the cooking time.
9. Let cool completely before serving.

Pecan And Cherry Stuffed Apples

Servings: 4
Cooking Time: 20 Minutes
Ingredients:
- 4 apples (about 565 g)
- 40 g chopped pecans
- 50 g dried tart cherries
- 1 tablespoon melted butter
- 3 tablespoons brown sugar
- ¼ teaspoon allspice
- Pinch salt
- Ice cream, for serving

Directions:
1. Cut off top ½ inch from each apple; reserve tops. With a melon baller, core through stem ends without breaking through the bottom.
2. Preheat the air fryer to 175°C. Combine pecans, cherries, butter, brown sugar, allspice, and a pinch of salt. Stuff mixture into the hollow centers of the apples. Cover with apple tops. Put in the air fryer basket, using tongs. Air fry for 20 to 25 minutes, or just until tender.
3. Serve warm with ice cream.

Gluten-free Spice Cookies

Servings: 4
Cooking Time: 12 Minutes
Ingredients:
- 4 tablespoons unsalted butter, at room temperature
- 2 tablespoons agave nectar
- 1 large egg
- 2 tablespoons water
- 240 g almond flour
- 100 g granulated sugar
- 2 teaspoons ground ginger
- 1 teaspoon ground cinnamon
- ½ teaspoon freshly grated nutmeg
- 1 teaspoon baking soda
- ¼ teaspoon kosher, or coarse sea salt

Directions:
1. Line the bottom of the air fryer basket with baking paper cut to fit.
2. In a large bowl, using a hand mixer, beat together the butter, agave, egg, and water on medium speed until light and fluffy.
3. Add the almond flour, sugar, ginger, cinnamon, nutmeg, baking soda, and salt. Beat on low speed until well combined.
4. Roll the dough into 2-tablespoon balls and arrange them on the baking paper in the basket. Set the air fryer to 165°C, and cook for 12 minutes, or until the tops of cookies are lightly browned.
5. Transfer to a wire rack and let cool completely. Store in an airtight container for up to a week.

Molten Chocolate Almond Cakes

Servings: 3
Cooking Time: 13 Minutes

Ingredients:
- Butter and flour for the ramekins
- 110 g bittersweet chocolate, chopped
- 110 gunsalted butter
- 2 eggs
- 2 egg yolks
- 50 g granulated sugar
- ½ teaspoon pure vanilla extract, or almond extract
- 1 tablespoon plain flour
- 3 tablespoons ground almonds
- 8 to 12 semisweet chocolate discs (or 4 chunks of chocolate)
- Cocoa powder or icing sugar, for dusting
- Toasted almonds, coarsely chopped

Directions:
1. Butter and flour three ramekins.
2. Melt the chocolate and butter together, either in the microwave or in a double boiler. In a separate bowl, beat the eggs, egg yolks and sugar together until light and smooth. Add the vanilla extract. Whisk the chocolate mixture into the egg mixture. Stir in the flour and ground almonds.
3. Preheat the air fryer to 165°C.
4. Transfer the batter carefully to the buttered ramekins, filling halfway. Place two or three chocolate discs in the center of the batter and then fill the ramekins to ½-inch below the top with the remaining batter. Place the ramekins into the zone 1 air fryer basket and air fry for 13 minutes. The sides of the cake should be set, but the centers should be slightly soft. Remove the ramekins from the air fryer and let the cakes sit for 5 minutes.
5. Run a butter knife around the edge of the ramekins and invert the cakes onto a plate. Lift the ramekin off the plate slowly and carefully so that the cake doesn't break. Dust with cocoa powder or icing sugar and serve with a scoop of ice cream and some coarsely chopped toasted almonds.

Stuffed Apples

Servings: 8
Cooking Time: 10 Minutes

Ingredients:
- 8 small firm apples, cored
- 1 cup golden raisins
- 1 cup blanched almonds
- 4 tablespoons sugar
- ¼ teaspoon ground cinnamon

Directions:
1. In a food processor, add raisins, almonds, sugar and cinnamon and pulse until chopped.
2. Carefully stuff each apple with raisin mixture.
3. Line each basket of "Zone 1" and "Zone 2" with parchment paper.
4. Press "Zone 1" and "Zone 2" and then rotate the knob for each zone to select "Air Fry".
5. Set the temperature to 355 degrees F/ 180 degrees C for both zones and then set the time for 5 minutes to preheat.
6. After preheating, arrange 4 apples into the basket of each zone.
7. Slide each basket into Air Fryer and set the time for 10 minutes.
8. After cooking time is completed, remove the apples from Air Fryer.
9. Transfer the apples onto plates and set aside to cool slightly before serving.

Homemade Mint Pie And Strawberry Pecan Pie

Servings: 8
Cooking Time: 25 Minutes
Ingredients:
- Homemade Mint Pie:
- 1 tablespoon instant coffee
- 2 tablespoons almond butter, softened
- 2 tablespoons granulated sweetener
- 1 teaspoon dried mint
- 3 eggs, beaten
- 1 teaspoon dried spearmint
- 4 teaspoons coconut flour
- Cooking spray
- Strawberry Pecan Pie:
- 190 g whole shelled pecans
- 1 tablespoon unsalted butter, softened
- 240 ml heavy whipping cream
- 12 medium fresh strawberries, hulled
- 2 tablespoons sour cream

Directions:
1. Make the Homemade Mint Pie:
2. Spray the zone 1 air fryer drawer with cooking spray.
3. Then mix all ingredients in the mixer bowl.
4. When you get a smooth mixture, transfer it in the zone 1 air fryer drawer. Flatten it gently. Cook the pie at 185ºC for 25 minutes.
5. Make the Strawberry Pecan Pie:
6. Place pecans and butter into a food processor and pulse ten times until a dough forms. Press dough into the bottom of an ungreased round nonstick baking dish.
7. Place dish into the zone 2 air fryer drawer. Adjust the temperature to 160ºC and set the timer for 10 minutes. Crust will be firm and golden when done. Let cool 20 minutes.
8. In a large bowl, whisk cream until fluffy and doubled in size, about 2 minutes.
9. In a separate large bowl, mash strawberries until mostly liquid. Fold strawberries and sour cream into whipped cream.
10. Spoon mixture into cooled crust, cover, and place in refrigerator for at least 30 minutes to set. Serve chilled.

Spiced Apple Cake

Servings: 6
Cooking Time: 30 Minutes
Ingredients:
- Vegetable oil
- 2 diced & peeled Gala apples
- 1 tablespoon fresh lemon juice
- 55 g unsalted butter, softened
- 65 g granulated sugar
- 2 large eggs
- 155 g plain flour
- 1½ teaspoons baking powder
- 1 tablespoon apple pie spice

- ½ teaspoon ground ginger
- ¼ teaspoon ground cardamom
- ¼ teaspoon ground nutmeg
- ½ teaspoon kosher, or coarse sea salt
- 60 ml whole milk
- Icing sugar, for dusting

Directions:
1. Grease a 0.7-liter Bundt, or tube pan with oil; set aside.
2. In a medium bowl, toss the apples with the lemon juice until well coated; set aside.
3. In a large bowl, combine the butter and sugar. Beat with an electric hand mixer on medium speed until the sugar has dissolved. Add the eggs and beat until fluffy. Add the flour, baking powder, apple pie spice, ginger, cardamom, nutmeg, salt, and milk. Mix until the batter is thick but pourable.
4. Pour the batter into the prepared pan. Top batter evenly with the apple mixture. Place the pan in the zone 1 air fryer drawer. Set the temperature to 176°C and cook for 30 minutes, or until a toothpick inserted in the center of the cake comes out clean. Close the air fryer and let the cake rest for 10 minutes. Turn the cake out onto a wire rack and cool completely.
5. Right before serving, dust the cake with icing sugar.

Butter Cake

Servings: 6
Cooking Time: 20 Minutes
Ingredients:
- 1 egg
- 3 tablespoons butter, softened
- ½ cup milk
- 1 tablespoon icing sugar
- ½ cup caster sugar
- 1½ cup plain flour
- A pinch of salt

Directions:
1. In a bowl, add the butter and sugar. Whisk until creamy.
2. Now, add the egg and whisk until fluffy.
3. Add the flour and salt. Mix well with the milk.
4. Place the mixture evenly into the greased cake pan.
5. Press "Zone 1" and "Zone 2" and then rotate the knob for each zone to select "Air Fry".
6. Set the temperature to 350 degrees F/ 175 degrees C for both zones and then set the time for 5 minutes to preheat.
7. After preheating, arrange the pan into the basket of each zone.
8. Slide each basket into Air Fryer and set the time for 15 minutes.
9. After cooking time is completed, remove the pan from Air Fryer.
10. Set aside to cool.
11. Serve and enjoy!

Mini Strawberry And Cream Pies

Servings: 2
Cooking Time: 15 Minutes
Ingredients:
- 1 box store-bought pie dough, Trader Joe's
- 1 cup strawberries, cubed
- 3 tablespoons cream, heavy
- 2 tablespoons almonds
- 1 egg white, for brushing

Directions:
1. Take the store-bought pie dough and flatten it on a surface.
2. Use a round cutter to cut it into 3-inch circles.
3. Brush the dough with egg white all around the edges.
4. Now add almonds, strawberries, and cream in a tiny amount in the center of the dough, and top it with another dough circle.
5. Press the edges with a fork to seal it.
6. Make a slit in the middle of the pie and divide them into the baskets.
7. Set zone 1 to AIR FRY mode 360 degrees F for 10 minutes.
8. Select MATCH for zone 2 basket.
9. Once done, serve.

Chocolate Chip Muffins

Servings: 2
Cooking Time: 15 Minutes
Ingredients:
- Salt, pinch
- 2 eggs
- ⅓ cup brown sugar
- ⅓ cup butter
- 4 tablespoons milk
- ¼ teaspoon vanilla extract
- ½ teaspoon baking powder
- 1 cup all-purpose flour
- 1 pouch chocolate chips, 35 grams

Directions:
1. Take 4 oven-safe ramekins that are the size of a cup and layer them with muffin papers.
2. In a bowl, with an electric beater mix the eggs, brown sugar, butter, milk, and vanilla extract.
3. In another bowl, mix the flour, baking powder, and salt.
4. Mix the dry into the wet slowly.
5. Fold in the chocolate chips and mix them in well.
6. Divide this batter into 4 ramekins and place them into both the baskets.
7. Set the time for zone 1 to 15 minutes at 350 degrees F on AIR FRY mode.
8. Select the MATCH button for the zone 2 basket.
9. If they are not completely done after 15 minutes, AIR FRY for another minute.
10. Once it is done, serve.

Jelly Donuts

Servings: 4
Cooking Time: 5 Minutes
Ingredients:
- 1 package Pillsbury Grands (Homestyle)
- ½ cup seedless raspberry jelly
- 1 tablespoon butter, melted
- ½ cup sugar

Directions:
1. Install a crisper plate in both drawers. Place half of the biscuits in the zone 1 drawer and half in zone 2's, then insert the drawers into the unit. You may need to cook in batches.
2. Select zone 1, select AIR FRY, set temperature to 390°F, and set time to 22 minutes. Select MATCH to match zone 2 settings to zone 1. Press the START/STOP button to begin cooking.
3. Place the sugar into a wide bowl with a flat bottom.
4. Baste all sides of the cooked biscuits with the melted butter and roll in the sugar to cover completely.
5. Using a long cake tip, pipe 1–2 tablespoons of raspberry jelly into each biscuit. You've now got raspberry-filled donuts!

Vegetables And Sides Recipes

Acorn Squash Slices

Servings: 6
Cooking Time: 10 Minutes
Ingredients:
- 2 medium acorn squashes
- ⅔ cup packed brown sugar
- ½ cup butter, melted

Directions:
1. Cut the squash in half, remove the seeds and slice into ½ inch slices.
2. Place the squash slices in the air fryer baskets.
3. Drizzle brown sugar and butter over the squash slices.
4. Return the air fryer basket 1 to Zone 1, and basket 2 to Zone 2 of the Ninja Foodi 2-Basket Air Fryer.
5. Choose the "Air Fry" mode for Zone 1 and set the temperature to 350 degrees F and 10 minutes of cooking time.
6. Select the "MATCH COOK" option to copy the settings for Zone 2.
7. Initiate cooking by pressing the START/PAUSE BUTTON.
8. Flip the squash once cooked halfway through.
9. Serve.

Nutrition:
- (Per serving) Calories 206 | Fat 3.4g |Sodium 174mg | Carbs 35g | Fiber 9.4g | Sugar 5.9g | Protein 10.6g

Quinoa Patties

Servings: 4
Cooking Time: 32 Minutes

Ingredients:
- 1 cup quinoa red
- 1½ cups water
- 1 teaspoon salt
- black pepper, ground
- 1½ cups rolled oats
- 3 eggs beaten
- ¼ cup minced white onion
- ½ cup crumbled feta cheese
- ¼ cup chopped fresh chives
- Salt and black pepper, to taste
- Vegetable or canola oil
- 4 hamburger buns
- 4 arugulas
- 4 slices tomato sliced
- Cucumber yogurt dill sauce
- 1 cup cucumber, diced
- 1 cup Greek yogurt
- 2 teaspoons lemon juice
- ¼ teaspoon salt
- Black pepper, ground
- 1 tablespoon chopped fresh dill
- 1 tablespoon olive oil

Directions:
1. Add quinoa to a saucepan filled with cold water, salt, and black pepper, and place it over medium-high heat.
2. Cook the quinoa to a boil, then reduce the heat, cover, and cook for 20 minutes on a simmer.
3. Fluff and mix the cooked quinoa with a fork and remove it from the heat.
4. Spread the quinoa in a baking stay.
5. Mix eggs, oats, onion, herbs, cheese, salt, and black pepper.
6. Stir in quinoa, then mix well. Make 4 patties out of this quinoa cheese mixture.
7. Divide the patties in the two crisper plates and spray them with cooking oil. 8. Return the crisper plates to the Ninja Foodi Dual Zone Air Fryer.
8. Choose the Air Fry mode for Zone 1 and set the temperature to 390 degrees F/ 200 degrees C and the time to 13 minutes.
9. Select the "MATCH" button to copy the settings for Zone 2.
10. Initiate cooking by pressing the START/STOP button.
11. Flip the patties once cooked halfway through, and resume cooking.
12. Meanwhile, prepare the cucumber yogurt dill sauce by mixing all of its ingredients in a mixing bowl.
13. Place each quinoa patty in a burger bun along with arugula leaves.
14. Serve with yogurt dill sauce.

Fried Olives

Servings: 6
Cooking Time: 9 Minutes
Ingredients:
- 2 cups blue cheese stuffed olives, drained
- ½ cup all-purpose flour
- 1 cup panko breadcrumbs
- ½ teaspoon garlic powder
- 1 pinch oregano
- 2 eggs

Directions:
1. Mix flour with oregano and garlic powder in a bowl and beat two eggs in another bowl.
2. Spread panko breadcrumbs in a bowl.
3. Coat all the olives with the flour mixture, dip in the eggs and then coat with the panko breadcrumbs.
4. As you coat the olives, place them in the two crisper plates in a single layer, then spray them with cooking oil.
5. Return the crisper plates to the Ninja Foodi Dual Zone Air Fryer.
6. Choose the Air Fry mode for Zone 1 and set the temperature to 375 degrees F/ 190 degrees C and the time to 9 minutes.
7. Select the "MATCH" button to copy the settings for Zone 2.
8. Initiate cooking by pressing the START/STOP button.
9. Flip the olives once cooked halfway through, then resume cooking.
10. Serve.

Garlic-rosemary Brussels Sprouts

Servings: 4
Cooking Time: 15 Minutes
Ingredients:
- 3 tablespoons olive oil
- 2 garlic cloves, minced
- ½ teaspoon salt
- ¼ teaspoon pepper
- 1-pound Brussels sprouts, trimmed and halved
- ½ cup panko breadcrumbs
- 1½ teaspoons minced fresh rosemary

Directions:
1. Place the first 4 ingredients in a small microwave-safe bowl| microwave on high for 30 seconds.
2. Toss the Brussels sprouts in 2 tablespoons of the microwaved mixture.
3. Place a crisper plate in each drawer. Put the sprouts in a single layer in each drawer. Insert the drawers into the units.
4. Select zone 1, then AIR FRY, then set the temperature to 360 degrees F/ 180 degrees C with a 6-minute timer. To match zone 2 settings to zone 1, choose MATCH. To begin, select START/STOP.
5. Remove the sprouts from the drawers after the timer has finished.
6. Toss the breadcrumbs with the rosemary and remaining oil mixture| sprinkle over the sprouts.
7. Continue cooking until the crumbs are browned, and the sprouts are tender. Serve immediately.

Balsamic Vegetables

Servings: 4
Cooking Time: 13 Minutes

Ingredients:
- 125g asparagus, cut woody ends
- 88g mushrooms, halved
- 1 tbsp Dijon mustard
- 3 tbsp soy sauce
- 27g brown sugar
- 57ml balsamic vinegar
- 32g olive oil
- 1 zucchini, sliced
- 1 yellow squash, sliced
- 170g grape tomatoes
- Pepper
- Salt

Directions:
1. In a bowl, mix asparagus, tomatoes, oil, mustard, soy sauce, mushrooms, zucchini, squash, brown sugar, vinegar, pepper, and salt.
2. Cover the bowl and place it in the refrigerator for 45 minutes.
3. Insert a crisper plate in the Ninja Foodi air fryer baskets.
4. Add the vegetable mixture in both baskets.
5. Select zone 1, then select "air fry" mode and set the temperature to 390 degrees F for 12 minutes. Press "match" to match zone 2 settings to zone 1. Press "start/stop" to begin. Stir halfway through.

Nutrition:
- (Per serving) Calories 184 | Fat 13.3g |Sodium 778mg | Carbs 14.7g | Fiber 3.6g | Sugar 9.5g | Protein 5.5g

Green Beans With Baked Potatoes

Servings: 2
Cooking Time: 45 Minutes

Ingredients:
- 2 cups green beans
- 2 large potatoes, cubed
- 3 tablespoons olive oil
- 1 teaspoon seasoned salt
- ½ teaspoon chili powder
- ⅙ teaspoon garlic powder
- ¼ teaspoon onion powder

Directions:
1. Take a large bowl and pour olive oil into it.
2. Add all the seasoning in the olive oil and whisk it well.
3. Toss the green beans in and mix well and then transfer to zone 1 basket of the air fryer.
4. Season the potatoes with the oil seasoning and add them to the zone 2 basket.
5. Press the Sync button.
6. Once the cooking cycle is complete, take out and serve.

Garlic-herb Fried Squash

Servings: 4
Cooking Time: 15 Minutes
Ingredients:
- 5 cups halved small pattypan squash (about 1¼ pounds)
- 1 tablespoon olive oil
- 2 garlic cloves, minced
- ½ teaspoon salt
- ¼ teaspoon dried oregano
- ¼ teaspoon dried thyme
- ¼ teaspoon pepper
- 1 tablespoon minced fresh parsley, for serving

Directions:
1. Place the squash in a large bowl.
2. Mix the oil, garlic, salt, oregano, thyme, and pepper| drizzle over the squash. Toss to coat.
3. Place a crisper plate in both drawers. Put the squash in a single layer in each drawer. Insert the drawers into the unit.
4. Select zone 1, then AIR FRY, then set the temperature to 360 degrees F/ 180 degrees C with a 6-minute timer. To match zone 2 settings to zone 1, choose MATCH. To begin, select START/STOP.
5. Remove the squash from the drawers after the timer has finished. Sprinkle with the parsley.

Garlic Herbed Baked Potatoes

Servings: 4
Cooking Time: 45 Minutes
Ingredients:
- 4 large baking potatoes
- Salt and black pepper, to taste
- 2 teaspoons avocado oil
- Cheese
- 2 cups sour cream
- 1 teaspoon garlic clove, minced
- 1 teaspoon fresh dill
- 2 teaspoons chopped chives
- Salt and black pepper, to taste
- 2 teaspoons Worcestershire sauce

Directions:
1. Pierce the skin of the potatoes with a fork.
2. Season the potatoes with olive oil, salt, and black pepper.
3. Divide the potatoes into the air fryer baskets.
4. Now press 1 for zone 1 and set it to AIR FRY mode at 350 degrees F/ 175 degrees C, for 45 minutes.
5. Select the MATCH button for zone 2.
6. Meanwhile, take a bowl and mix all the cheese ingredients together.
7. Once the cooking cycle is complete, take out the potatoes and make a slit in-between each one.
8. Add the cheese mixture in the cavity and serve it hot.

Fried Avocado Tacos

Servings: 4
Cooking Time: 10 Minutes
Ingredients:
- For the sauce:
- 2 cups shredded fresh kale or coleslaw mix
- ¼ cup minced fresh cilantro
- ¼ cup plain Greek yogurt
- 2 tablespoons lime juice
- 1 teaspoon honey
- ¼ teaspoon salt
- ¼ teaspoon ground chipotle pepper
- ¼ teaspoon pepper
- For the tacos:
- 1 large egg, beaten
- ¼ cup cornmeal
- ½ teaspoon salt
- ½ teaspoon garlic powder
- ½ teaspoon ground chipotle pepper
- 2 medium avocados, peeled and sliced
- Cooking spray
- 8 flour tortillas or corn tortillas (6 inches), heated up
- 1 medium tomato, chopped
- Crumbled queso fresco (optional)

Directions:
1. Combine the first 8 ingredients in a bowl. Cover and refrigerate until serving.
2. Place the egg in a shallow bowl. In another shallow bowl, mix the cornmeal, salt, garlic powder, and chipotle pepper.
3. Dip the avocado slices in the egg, then into the cornmeal mixture, gently patting to help adhere.
4. Place a crisper plate in both drawers. Put the avocado slices in the drawers in a single layer. Insert the drawers into the unit.
5. Select zone 1, then AIR FRY, then set the temperature to 360 degrees F/ 180 degrees C with a 6-minute timer. To match zone 2 settings to zone 1, choose MATCH. To begin, select START/STOP.
6. Put the avocado slices, prepared sauce, tomato, and queso fresco in the tortillas and serve.

Falafel

Servings: 6
Cooking Time: 14 Minutes
Ingredients:
- 1 (15.5-oz) can chickpeas, rinsed and drained
- 1 small yellow onion, cut into quarters
- 3 garlic cloves, chopped
- ⅓ cup parsley, chopped
- ⅓ cup cilantro, chopped
- ⅓ cup scallions, chopped
- 1 teaspoon cumin
- ½ teaspoons salt

- ⅛ teaspoons crushed red pepper flakes
- 1 teaspoon baking powder
- 4 tablespoons all-purpose flour
- Olive oil spray

Directions:
1. Dry the chickpeas on paper towels.
2. Add onions and garlic to a food processor and chop them.
3. Add the parsley, salt, cilantro, scallions, cumin, and red pepper flakes.
4. Press the pulse button for 60 seconds, then toss in chickpeas and blend for 3 times until it makes a chunky paste.
5. Stir in baking powder and flour and mix well.
6. Transfer the falafel mixture to a bowl and cover to refrigerate for 3 hours.
7. Make 12 balls out of the falafel mixture.
8. Place 6 falafels in each of the crisper plate and spray them with oil.
9. Return the crisper plate to the Ninja Foodi Dual Zone Air Fryer.
10. Choose the Air Fry mode for Zone 1 and set the temperature to 350 degrees F/ 175 degrees C and the time to 14 minutes.
11. Select the "MATCH" button to copy the settings for Zone 2.
12. Initiate cooking by pressing the START/STOP button.
13. Toss the falafel once cooked halfway through, and resume cooking.
14. Serve warm.

Flavourful Mexican Cauliflower

Servings: 4
Cooking Time: 12 Minutes

Ingredients:
- 1 medium cauliflower head, cut into florets
- ½ tsp turmeric
- 1 tsp onion powder
- 2 tsp garlic powder
- 2 tsp parsley
- 1 lime juice
- 30ml olive oil
- 1 tsp chilli powder
- 1 tsp cumin
- Pepper
- Salt

Directions:
1. In a bowl, toss cauliflower florets with onion powder, garlic powder, parsley, oil, chilli powder, turmeric, cumin, pepper, and salt.
2. Insert a crisper plate in the Ninja Foodi air fryer baskets.
3. Add cauliflower florets in both baskets.
4. Select zone 1, then select "air fry" mode and set the temperature to 390 degrees F for 12 minutes. Press "match" to match zone 2 settings to zone 1. Press "start/stop" to begin. Stir halfway through.
5. Drizzle lime juice over cauliflower florets.

Nutrition:
- (Per serving) Calories 108 | Fat 7.4g |Sodium 91mg | Carbs 10g | Fiber 4.1g | Sugar 4.1g | Protein 3.4g

Stuffed Tomatoes

Servings: 2
Cooking Time: 8 Minutes

Ingredients:

- 2 cups brown rice, cooked
- 1 cup tofu, grilled and chopped
- 4 large red tomatoes
- 4 tablespoons basil, chopped
- ¼ tablespoon olive oil
- Salt and black pepper, to taste
- 2 tablespoons lemon juice
- 1 teaspoon red chili powder
- ½ cup Parmesan cheese

Directions:

1. Take a large bowl and mix rice, tofu, basil, olive oil, salt, black pepper, lemon juice, and chili powder.
2. Core the center of the tomatoes.
3. Fill the cavity with the rice mixture.
4. Top them off with the cheese sprinkle.
5. Divide the tomatoes into two air fryer baskets.
6. Turn zone 1 to AIR FRY mode for 8 minutes at 400 degrees F/ 200 degrees C.
7. Select the MATCH button for zone 2.
8. Serve and enjoy.

Broccoli, Squash, & Pepper

Servings: 4
Cooking Time: 12 Minutes

Ingredients:

- 175g broccoli florets
- 1 red bell pepper, diced
- 1 tbsp olive oil
- ½ tsp garlic powder
- ¼ onion, sliced
- 1 zucchini, sliced
- 2 yellow squash, sliced
- Pepper
- Salt

Directions:

1. In a bowl, toss veggies with oil, garlic powder, pepper, and salt.
2. Insert a crisper plate in the Ninja Foodi air fryer baskets.
3. Add the vegetable mixture in both baskets.
4. Select zone 1 then select "air fry" mode and set the temperature to 390 degrees F for 12 minutes. Press "match" to match zone 2 settings to zone 1. Press "start/stop" to begin. Stir halfway through.

Nutrition:

- (Per serving) Calories 75 | Fat 3.9g |Sodium 62mg | Carbs 9.6g | Fiber 2.8g | Sugar 4.8g | Protein 2.9g

Satay-style Tempeh With Corn Fritters

Servings: 4
Cooking Time: 15 Minutes

Ingredients:
- FOR THE TEMPEH
- 1 (8-ounce) package tempeh
- 3 tablespoons fresh lemon juice, divided
- 2 tablespoons soy sauce, divided
- 2 garlic cloves, chopped
- ½ teaspoon ground turmeric
- 2 tablespoons vegetable oil
- ¾ cup canned full-fat coconut milk
- 4 tablespoons peanut butter
- 1 teaspoon light brown sugar
- ½ teaspoon red pepper flakes
- 1 scallion, chopped
- FOR THE CORN FRITTERS
- 2 cups frozen corn, thawed and drained
- 2 scallions, thinly sliced
- ¼ cup chopped fresh cilantro
- ¼ teaspoon kosher salt
- 2 large eggs
- ½ cup all-purpose flour
- 2 tablespoons vegetable oil

Directions:
1. To prep the tempeh: Slice the tempeh into ¼-inch-thick slabs.
2. In a large bowl, combine 2 tablespoons of lemon juice, 1 tablespoon of soy sauce, the garlic, turmeric, and oil.
3. Add the tempeh to the marinade and toss to coat the pieces. Let marinate for 15 minutes.
4. In a medium bowl, whisk together the coconut milk, peanut butter, remaining 1 tablespoon of lemon juice, remaining 1 tablespoon of soy sauce, brown sugar, red pepper flakes, and scallion. Set aside.
5. To prep the corn fritters: In a large bowl, combine the corn, scallions, cilantro, and salt. Mix in the eggs and flour until everything is well combined.
6. To cook the tempeh and fritters: Install a broil rack in the Zone 1 basket. Arrange the tempeh in a single layer on the rack and insert the basket in the unit. Install a crisper plate in the Zone 2 basket. Spoon 2 tablespoons of corn fritter batter into each corner of the basket and drizzle with oil. Flatten slightly with the back of the spoon and insert the basket in the unit.
7. Select Zone 1, select AIR BROIL, set the temperature to 400°F, and set the timer to 8 minutes.
8. Select Zone 2, select AIR FRY, set the temperature to 375°F, and set the timer to 15 minutes. Select SMART FINISH.
9. Press START/PAUSE to begin cooking.
10. When the Zone 2 timer reads 5 minutes, press START/PAUSE. Remove the basket and use silicone-tipped tongs or a spatula to flip the corn fritters. Reinsert the basket and press START/PAUSE to resume cooking.
11. When cooking is complete, the tempeh will be golden brown and the corn fritters set in the center and browned on the edges.
12. Serve the tempeh with the peanut sauce for dipping and the corn fritters on the side.

Nutrition:
- (Per serving) Calories: 578; Total fat: 40g; Saturated fat: 14g; Carbohydrates: 39g; Fiber: 3.5g; Protein: 24g; Sodium: 815mg

Fried Patty Pan Squash

Servings: 6
Cooking Time: 15 Minutes

Ingredients:
- 5 cups small pattypan squash, halved
- 1 tablespoon olive oil
- 2 garlic cloves, minced
- ½ teaspoon salt
- ¼ teaspoon dried oregano
- ¼ teaspoon dried thyme
- ¼ teaspoon pepper
- 1 tablespoon minced parsley

Directions:
1. Rub the squash with oil, garlic and the rest of the ingredients.
2. Spread the squash in the air fryer baskets.
3. Return the air fryer basket 1 to Zone 1, and basket 2 to Zone 2 of the Ninja Foodi 2-Basket Air Fryer.
4. Choose the "Air Fry" mode for Zone 1 at 375 degrees F and 15 minutes of cooking time.
5. Select the "MATCH COOK" option to copy the settings for Zone 2.
6. Initiate cooking by pressing the START/PAUSE BUTTON.
7. Flip the squash once cooked halfway through.
8. Garnish with parsley.
9. Serve warm.

Nutrition:
- (Per serving) Calories 208 | Fat 5g | Sodium 1205mg | Carbs 34.1g | Fiber 7.8g | Sugar 2.5g | Protein 5.9g

Air-fried Radishes

Servings: 6
Cooking Time: 15 Minutes

Ingredients:
- 1020g radishes, quartered
- 3 tablespoons olive oil
- 1 tablespoon fresh oregano, minced
- ¼ teaspoon salt
- ⅛ teaspoon black pepper

Directions:
1. Toss radishes with oil, black pepper, salt and oregano in a bowl.
2. Divide the radishes into the Ninja Foodi 2 Baskets Air Fryer baskets.
3. Return the air fryer basket 1 to Zone 1, and basket 2 to Zone 2 of the Ninja Foodi 2-Basket Air Fryer.
4. Choose the "Air Fry" mode for Zone 1 at 375 degrees F and 15 minutes of cooking time.
5. Select the "MATCH COOK" option to copy the settings for Zone 2.
6. Initiate cooking by pressing the START/PAUSE BUTTON.
7. Toss the radishes once cooked halfway through.
8. Serve.

Nutrition:
- (Per serving) Calories 270 | Fat 14.6g | Sodium 394mg | Carbs 31.3g | Fiber 7.5g | Sugar 9.7g | Protein 6.4g

Green Tomato Stacks

Servings: 6
Cooking Time: 12 Minutes

Ingredients:
- ¼ cup mayonnaise
- ¼ teaspoon lime zest, grated
- 2 tablespoons lime juice
- 1 teaspoon minced fresh thyme
- ½ teaspoon black pepper
- ¼ cup all-purpose flour
- 2 large egg whites, beaten
- ¾ cup cornmeal
- ¼ teaspoon salt
- 2 medium green tomatoes
- 2 medium re tomatoes
- Cooking spray
- 8 slices Canadian bacon, warmed

Directions:
1. Mix mayonnaise with ¼ teaspoon black pepper, thyme, lime juice and zest in a bowl.
2. Spread flour in one bowl, beat egg whites in another bowl and mix cornmeal with ¼ teaspoon black pepper and salt in a third bowl.
3. Cut the tomatoes into 4 slices and coat each with the flour then dip in the egg whites.
4. Coat the tomatoes slices with the cornmeal mixture.
5. Place the slices in the air fryer baskets.
6. Return the air fryer basket 1 to Zone 1, and basket 2 to Zone 2 of the Ninja Foodi 2-Basket Air Fryer.
7. Choose the "Air Fry" mode for Zone 1 at 390 degrees F and 12 minutes of cooking time.
8. Select the "MATCH COOK" option to copy the settings for Zone 2.
9. Initiate cooking by pressing the START/PAUSE BUTTON.
10. Flip the tomatoes once cooked halfway through.
11. Place the green tomato slices on the working surface.
12. Top them with bacon, and red tomato slice.
13. Serve.

Nutrition:
- (Per serving) Calories 113 | Fat 3g |Sodium 152mg | Carbs 20g | Fiber 3g | Sugar 1.1g | Protein 3.5g

Buffalo Seitan With Crispy Zucchini Noodles

Servings:4
Cooking Time: 12 Minutes

Ingredients:
- FOR THE BUFFALO SEITAN
- 1 (8-ounce) package precooked seitan strips
- 1 teaspoon garlic powder, divided
- ½ teaspoon onion powder
- ¼ teaspoon smoked paprika
- ¼ cup Louisiana-style hot sauce
- 2 tablespoons vegetable oil
- 1 tablespoon tomato paste
- ¼ teaspoon freshly ground black pepper

- FOR THE ZUCCHINI NOODLES
- 3 large egg whites
- 1¼ cups all-purpose flour
- 1 teaspoon kosher salt, divided
- 12 ounces seltzer water or club soda
- 5 ounces zucchini noodles
- Nonstick cooking spray

Directions:
1. To prep the Buffalo seitan: Season the seitan strips with ½ teaspoon of garlic powder, the onion powder, and smoked paprika.
2. In a large bowl, whisk together the hot sauce, oil, tomato paste, remaining ½ teaspoon of garlic powder, and the black pepper. Set the bowl of Buffalo sauce aside.
3. To prep the zucchini noodles: In a medium bowl, use a handheld mixer to beat the egg whites until stiff peaks form.
4. In a large bowl, combine the flour and ½ teaspoon of salt. Mix in the seltzer to form a thin batter. Fold in the beaten egg whites.
5. Add the zucchini to the batter and gently mix to coat.
6. To cook the seitan and zucchini noodles: Install a crisper plate in each of the two baskets. Place the seitan in the Zone 1 basket and insert the basket in the unit. Lift the noodles from the batter one at a time, letting the excess drip off, and place them in the Zone 2 basket. Insert the basket in the unit.
7. Select Zone 1, select BAKE, set the temperature to 370°F, and set the timer to 12 minutes.
8. Select Zone 2, select AIR FRY, set the temperature to 400°F, and set the timer to 12 minutes. Select SMART FINISH.
9. Press START/PAUSE to begin cooking.
10. When the Zone 1 timer reads 2 minutes, press START/PAUSE. Remove the basket and transfer the seitan to the bowl of Buffalo sauce. Turn to coat, then return the seitan to the basket. Reinsert the basket and press START/PAUSE to resume cooking.
11. When cooking is complete, the seitan should be warmed through and the zucchini noodles crisp and light golden brown.
12. Sprinkle the zucchini noodles with the remaining ½ teaspoon of salt. If desired, drizzle extra Buffalo sauce over the seitan. Serve hot.

Nutrition:
- (Per serving) Calories: 252; Total fat: 15g; Saturated fat: 1g; Carbohydrates: 22g; Fiber: 1.5g; Protein: 13g; Sodium: 740mg

Chickpea Fritters

Servings: 6
Cooking Time: 6 Minutes

Ingredients:
- 237ml plain yogurt
- 2 tablespoons sugar
- 1 tablespoon honey
- ½ teaspoon salt
- ½ teaspoon black pepper
- ½ teaspoon crushed red pepper flakes
- 1 can (28g) chickpeas, drained
- 1 teaspoon ground cumin
- ½ teaspoon salt
- ½ teaspoon garlic powder

- ½ teaspoon ground ginger
- 1 large egg
- ½ teaspoon baking soda
- ½ cup fresh coriander, chopped
- 2 green onions, sliced

Directions:
1. Mash chickpeas with rest of the ingredients in a food processor.
2. Layer the two air fryer baskets with a parchment paper.
3. Drop the batter in the baskets spoon by spoon.
4. Return the air fryer basket 1 to Zone 1, and basket 2 to Zone 2 of the Ninja Foodi 2-Basket Air Fryer.
5. Choose the "Air Fry" mode for Zone 1 at 400 degrees F and 6 minutes of cooking time.
6. Select the "MATCH COOK" option to copy the settings for Zone 2.
7. Initiate cooking by pressing the START/PAUSE BUTTON.
8. Flip the fritters once cooked halfway through.
9. Serve warm.

Nutrition:
- (Per serving) Calories 284 | Fat 7.9g | Sodium 704mg | Carbs 38.1g | Fiber 1.9g | Sugar 1.9g | Protein 14.8g

Air Fryer Vegetables

Servings: 2
Cooking Time: 15 Minutes

Ingredients:
- 1 courgette, diced
- 2 capsicums, diced
- 1 head broccoli, diced
- 1 red onion, diced
- Marinade
- 1 teaspoon smoked paprika
- 1 teaspoon garlic granules
- 1 teaspoon Herb de Provence
- Salt and black pepper, to taste
- 1½ tablespoon olive oil
- 2 tablespoons lemon juice

Directions:
1. Toss the veggies with the rest of the marinade ingredients in a bowl.
2. Spread the veggies in the air fryer baskets.
3. Return the air fryer basket 1 to Zone 1, and basket 2 to Zone 2 of the Ninja Foodi 2-Basket Air Fryer.
4. Choose the "Air Fry" mode for Zone 1 at 400 degrees F and 15 minutes of cooking time.
5. Select the "MATCH COOK" option to copy the settings for Zone 2.
6. Initiate cooking by pressing the START/PAUSE BUTTON.
7. Toss the veggies once cooked half way through.
8. Serve warm.

Nutrition:
- (Per serving) Calories 166 | Fat 3.2g | Sodium 437mg | Carbs 28.8g | Fiber 1.8g | Sugar 2.7g | Protein 5.8g

RECIPES INDEX

A

Acorn Squash Slices 92
Air Fried Bananas 85
Air Fryer Calamari 36
Air Fryer Vegetables 104
Air-fried Radishes 101
Almond Chicken 50
Apple Crumble 84
Asian Chicken Drumsticks 46
Asian Glazed Meatballs 69

B

Bacon And Eggs For Breakfast 22
Bacon Cheese Egg With Avocado And Potato Nuggets 21
Bacon Cinnamon Rolls 12
Bacon Wrapped Pork Tenderloin 66
Bacon-and-eggs Avocado And Simple Scotch Eggs 17
Balsamic Vegetables 95
Bbq Cheddar-stuffed Chicken Breasts 47
Beef Jerky Pineapple Jerky 78
Beef Skewers 75
Berry Crumble And S'mores 85
Breakfast Frittata 22
Breakfast Sausage And Cauliflower 19
Breakfast Stuffed Peppers 11
Broccoli, Squash, & Pepper 99
Broccoli-mushroom Frittata And Chimichanga Breakfast Burrito 16

Brussels Sprouts Potato Hash 14
Buffalo Chicken 52
Buffalo Seitan With Crispy Zucchini Noodles 102
Butter Cake 90

C

Cajun Breakfast Sausage 15
Caramelized Onion Dip With White Cheese 82
Cheese Corn Fritters 80
Cheese Stuffed Mushrooms 76
Cheesesteak Taquitos 64
Cheesy Baked Eggs 13
Chicken & Broccoli 55
Chicken Bites 54
Chicken Crescent Wraps 76
Chicken Stuffed Mushrooms 80
Chicken Thighs In Waffles 56
Chickpea Fritters 103
Chili Lime Tilapia 41
Chipotle Drumsticks 53
Chocó Lava Cake 84
Chocolate Chip Muffins 91
Chorizo And Beef Burger 62
Cod With Jalapeño 39
Cornish Hen With Asparagus 57
Cornish Hen With Baked Potatoes 47
Crab Cake Poppers 81
Crispy Filo Artichoke Triangles 78
Crispy Parmesan Cod 27

Crispy Ranch Nuggets 51

Crumbed Chicken Katsu 45

Crumb-topped Sole 34

Crusted Chicken Breast 52

D

Delicious Apple Fritters 83

Donuts 23

Double-dipped Mini Cinnamon Biscuits 15

Dukkah-crusted Halibut 28

E

Easy Cajun Chicken Drumsticks 56

Easy Herbed Salmon 26

Easy Sausage Pizza 21

F

Falafel 97

Fish Fillets With Lemon-dill Sauce 31

Fish Sandwich 31

Flavourful Mexican Cauliflower 98

French Toast Sticks 19

Fried Avocado Tacos 97

Fried Cheese 72

Fried Olives 94

Fried Patty Pan Squash 101

Furikake Salmon 37

G

Garlic Herbed Baked Potatoes 96

Garlic-herb Fried Squash 96

Garlic-rosemary Brussels Sprouts 94

Gluten-free Spice Cookies 87

Greek Chicken Meatballs 51

Greek Chicken Souvlaki 54

Green Beans With Baked Potatoes 95

Green Tomato Stacks 102

H

Ham Burger Patties 71

Harissa-rubbed Chicken 48

Hawaiian Chicken Bites 55

Healthy Chickpea Fritters 82

Healthy Spinach Balls 77

Herb Lemon Mussels 27

Homemade Mint Pie And Strawberry Pecan Pie 89

Homemade Toaster Pastries 14

Honey Butter Chicken 44

Honey Teriyaki Tilapia 30

I

Indian Fennel Chicken 49

Italian Sausages With Peppers And Teriyaki Rump Steak With Broccoli 67

J

Jalapeño Popper Chicken 77

Jelly Donuts 92

K

Keto Baked Salmon With Pesto 33

L

Lamb Chops With Dijon Garlic 62

M

Marinated Pork Chops 69

Mexican Jalapeno Poppers 81

Mini Blueberry Pies 86

Mini Strawberry And Cream Pies 91

Miso Salmon And Oyster Po'boy 43

Mojito Lamb Chops 59

Molten Chocolate Almond Cakes 88

Mozzarella Stuffed Beef And Pork Meatballs 65

Mushroom-and-tomato Stuffed Hash Browns 23

N

Nutty Prawns With Amaretto Glaze 37

O

Onion Omelette And Buffalo Egg Cups 24

Oyster Po'boy 42

P

Parmesan Pork Chops 70

Pecan And Cherry Stuffed Apples 87

Pecan Brownies And Cinnamon-sugar Almonds 86

Pecan-crusted Catfish Nuggets With "fried" Okra 41

Pecan-crusted Chicken Tenders 45

Pork Chops With Brussels Sprouts 64

Pork Sausage Eggs With Mustard Sauce 20

Pork With Green Beans And Potatoes 72

Potato Chips 74

Prawns Curry And Paprika Crab Burgers 38

Pretzels Hot Dog 73

Puff Pastry 18

Q

Quick And Easy Blueberry Muffins 16

Quinoa Patties 93

R

Rainbow Salmon Kebabs And Tuna Melt 28

Ranch Turkey Tenders With Roasted Vegetable Salad 48

Red Pepper And Feta Frittata 20

Roast Beef 70

Rosemary Ribeye Steaks And Mongolian-style Beef 61

S

Salmon Nuggets 35

Salmon Patties 39

Satay-style Tempeh With Corn Fritters 100

Sausage And Egg Breakfast Burrito 24

Sausage With Eggs 13

Scallops Gratiné With Parmesan 40

Scallops With Greens 34

Seasoned Tuna Steaks 44

Simple Buttery Cod & Salmon On Bed Of Fennel And Carrot 30

Smothered Chops 66

Spiced Apple Cake 89

Spice-rubbed Pork Loin 60

Spicy Lamb Chops 68

Spinach And Swiss Frittata With Mushrooms 18

Steak And Asparagus Bundles 60

Steak Fajitas With Onions And Peppers 68

Steak In Air Fry 71

Steaks With Walnut-blue Cheese Butter 65

Strawberries And Walnuts Muffins 74

Stuffed Apples 88

Stuffed Beef Fillet With Feta Cheese 59

Stuffed Chicken Florentine 46

Stuffed Tomatoes 99

Sweet Potato Donut Holes 83

Sweet Potato Hash 12

Sweet Potato Sausage Hash 25

T

Taco-spiced Chickpeas And Black Bean Corn Dip 79

Tandoori Prawns 33

Tasty Lamb Patties 63

Tex-mex Chicken Roll-ups 50

Thai Chicken Meatballs 53

Thai Prawn Skewers And Lemon-tarragon Fish En Papillote 35

Tilapia With Mojo And Crispy Plantains 32

Tomahawk Steak 63

Tuna With Herbs 40

Turkey Meatloaf With Veggie Medley 58

W

Waffle Fries 73

Wholemeal Banana-walnut Bread 26

Y

Yellow Potatoes With Eggs 11

Yummy Chicken Breasts 57

Z

Zucchini Chips 75

Printed in Great Britain
by Amazon

47268693R00064